WOKERY: A WAKE-UP CALL FOR THE WEST

WOKERY: A WAKE-UP CALL FOR THE WEST

Proceedings of the
Christopher Dawson Centre Colloquium 2023

edited by David Daintree

Christopher Dawson Press
Hobart, Tasmania, Australia
2024

The Christopher Dawson Centre for Cultural Studies
35 Tower Road
New Town
Tasmania 7008
Australia

www.dawsoncentre.org

ISBN: 978-0-6455993-1-2

ACKNOWLEDGEMENTS

Layout and cover design by Eilidh Direen

Cover image: *Massacre of the Innocents* by Pieter Bruegel the Elder. British Royal Collection, c. 1565-67.

Contents

INTRODUCTION
David Daintree

The theme we chose for our eighth annual Colloquium was a problem from the outset. *Wokery: a Wake-Up Call for the West* could win no prizes for diplomacy or tact. We were clearly going to confront what we saw as dangerous, potentially fatal fissures in the fabric of society. The situation worsened because of the following statement which I indiscreetly included in our original call for papers:

'school children are taught to believe that girls can be boys, that boys can be girls, and that grown-ups should be punished for denying it.'

Jane Franklin Hall, the college of the University of Tasmania where we had held all our earlier colloquia, consequently advised us that it was no longer willing to host us. This was a bitter blow. I have some sympathy for the college's administration because I know and admire the Principal and her staff. I understand that they want to protect transitioning students from possible hurt, but I radically disagree with their strategy. I believe that such people do not need - and should not expect - the silencing of opinions that conflict with their own. We must not cocoon them in cotton wool. People on the threshold of making life-changing decisions should be

7

able to access arguments for and against. A 'woke' society, with its strong inclination to silence unwelcome views rather than defend the merits of its own in open forum, is incapable of protecting the freedoms of its members. Worse than incapable: unwilling.

If one believes that too many young people are making life-changing decisions too readily, without weighing up all the evidence, and if one believes that the post-war generation and the one that followed have been remiss in walking away from the responsibilities of parenthood, then one is bound in conscience to speak up. We could not contemplate a situation in which any of the Centre's activities would submit to the need for an external *imprimatur*, so we didn't argue the toss, but rolled over with a good grace and found a welcoming alternative venue - the Italian Club in North Hobart.

So-called Freedom of Speech is actually problematic. We all approve of it in principle. The view that some people (Conservatives? Right-wingers?) are in favour of it and others (Liberals? The Left?) are against is altogether too facile. Nobody speaks against it, but the reality that nobody, simply nobody, believes in complete freedom of speech is easily tested: fearlessly question your most tolerant and easy-going friends and it won't take long to discover subjects that all regard as beyond the pale!

Consequently we should not feel embarrassed if we believe that some restriction on what is said and written in public might be a moral imperative, though years of liberalism since the 60s, of which the overturning of the ban on *Lady Chatterley's Lover* was almost an icon, have inured almost all of us, left as well as right, to a pretty easy-going tolerance of virtually anything. Raised and nurtured in the supposedly enlightened 1960s, with its mantra 'let it all hang out', we feel uncomfortable about any impulse towards censorship.

But the Left of today is very different from the Left of 60 years ago. There is little in common but the name. The old Left was certainly repressive, as those of us who tried to express a contrary opinion at student meetings can well remember, but there was a difference: we all believed in freedom of speech even if we shouted each other down, we even liked one another up to a point, or so it seems with the kindly benefit of hindsight.

Currently that amorphous group commonly known as The Left that holds most of the power in politics, media and public opinion is far from being the old Left of decades ago. Radical reform of society in such areas as race, gender, identity, religion and climate is high on their agenda. Opponents of their plans are viewed with more than mere mistrust; their opinions are often labelled *misinformation* or *disinformation* - such subtle distinctions - and risk being silenced. They are quick to accuse those who stand in their way of hate speech, but their own actions are obviously driven by hate and malice.

The awful truth that conservatives must face is that those on the political Right are often no better. They too are heirs of the 60s. Having for the most part abandoned religion with almost the same alacrity as the Left they have no tolerance for Christian exceptionalism, particularly when it relates to sexual morality. This is why the parties and groups once considered conservative have so comprehensively betrayed those who are genuinely conservative. Dan Andrews was re-elected in Victoria because the alternative Liberal leader was merely a weaker imitation. Years of Liberal government federally saw the appointment of left-leaning progressives in almost every area of public life. There is a kind of moral bankruptcy where we would hope to find strong ethical leadership.

Are true conservatives any better? Sadly, probably not. When they get the upper hand many are liable to use it just as ruthlessly as anybody else. Examples of historical misuse of power are legion - on both sides of the progressive/ conservative divide. It is both honest and wise to be conscious of this. Perhaps recognising this shared human inclination to block opposing opinions should heighten our respect for at least some of the motives of those who would silence us, and also make us less inclined passively to bewail our own victimhood and more willing to go bravely to the barricades in defence of our beliefs.

Those who spoke at our Colloquium impressed us with their strength and courage. They accused nobody of 'hate speech', that most repulsive charge, a foul and cheap jibe so glibly used by activists on both sides when actual evidence is unavailable. They just got on with it, argued their cases with cogency and eloquence, and provided us with as rich a lode of wisdom as we have ever had the privilege of putting together in one volume.

I thank them all and warmly commend their work to you.

THE PLACE OF DEBATE IN AUSTRALIAN EDUCATION: FORTIFYING A FREE AND CIVIL SOCIETY

Deidre Clary and Fiona Mueller

ABSTRACT

Taught well, students can learn to debate important issues in ways that enhance their cognitive, intellectual, linguistic, academic and social skills, with profound advantages for post-school study, work and life, and – ideally – for the nation. Australian school education is guided by documents such as the Alice Springs (Mparntwe) Declaration (2019). Like its three predecessors, that Declaration identifies an overarching goal of helping young Australians to become 'active and informed citizens'. The capacity to debate important issues on the basis of sound research and reason is the essence of a free and civil society. Active and informed citizens need to appreciate the origins and purpose of debate, including the extent to which it reflects the development of Western and Christian values and beliefs such as freedom of speech, individualism, the pursuit of truth, and the rule of law. The art of debating is not a distinctive feature of the Australian Curriculum, nor is it commonly taught in schools. Few teachers have the expertise and skills to model effective debating or to facilitate the process. This paper will focus on the importance of debate and consider current tensions between a knowledge-based curriculum and the so-called 21st century learning agenda.

The title of our paper – *The place of debate in Australian education: fortifying a free and civil society* – reflects our concern about the diminishing role of some traditional methods of teaching and learning designed to cement knowledge and enhance cognitive and linguistic skills. Debating has long been one such method.

Galloping along new technological paths, including the high-profile tracks of artificial intelligence, extended reality, robotics and online learning, allows little time to consider what to keep and what to let go.

We assert that some approaches to teaching and learning – as last century or last millennium as they may seem – remain central to the formation of citizens who can contribute confidently and articulately to a free and civil society. Debating is part of an intellectual and socio-political tradition that encourages both linguistic dexterity and thoughtful participation in the democratic process.

Our professional observation is that there is an ongoing generational decline in Australians' competence in the English language. We believe there has been a loss of emphasis on the association between the development of sophisticated English language skills, including the capacity and willingness to read regularly and widely, and the requirement for students to undertake rigorous research and produce reasoned arguments (either oral or written) on the basis of evidence.

Others have presented in this forum about the importance of free speech and debate. At the Christopher Dawson Centre's 2022 Colloquium, Dr David van Gend was unequivocal.[1]

1   van Gend, D. (2022) 'Citizens of no mean city.' 7th Colloquium - The Christopher Dawson Centre for Cultural Studies. Hobart

Free speech – which means free argument – is the expression of free thought, and the thoughts that matter most to individuals are those formed out of deep, conscientious struggle. Without free thought and free argument, we are not free citizens, or even free souls. We lose the capacity to defend our deepest convictions and therefore lose the essence of our humanity, which is to live according to what we judge to be true and right. Free speech – which means free argument – is at the heart of a society that settles its disputes by debate, not by guns.

Learning to settle disputes by debate, we maintain, should be at the heart of education.

The post-pandemic socio-political context in which Australia finds itself should stimulate national debate as never before. Key issues include Indigenous representation in Parliament, national security and defence, cost of living, energy supply, health, workforce planning and productivity, immigration, and the list goes on and on.

The Australian Curriculum, the national document that 'sets the expectations for what all young Australians should be taught'[2] claims that:

Education plays a critical role in shaping the lives of young Australians and contributing to a democratic, equitable and just society that is prosperous, cohesive and culturally diverse.

A democratic, equitable and just society places debate at the heart of decision-making, ensuring that all possible perspectives may be heard.

2   ACARA. (2023) Australian Curriculum (Version 9.0) https://www.australiancurriculum.edu.au/about-the-australian-curriculum/

However, in contemporary Australian education, the place occupied by debate is so minor as to be a case of blink and you will miss it.

In part, at least, this is due to new movements in education.

Across the world, curriculum development is increasingly dominated by the so-called 21st century learning agenda, which prioritises skills, dispositions and attributes deemed essential to 'navigating' post-school life and work. With its relentless focus on the future, it can be difficult to see how this agenda, centering around technology and globalism, can ensure that Australian educators address longstanding academic deficits.

Despite the excitement surrounding international millennium goals for education, the publication of Australian education 'roadmaps' such as the Alice Springs (Mparntwe) Declaration and the significant increase in annual taxpayer expenditure on schooling in recent decades, too few students are thriving academically.

There is an unhelpful tension between the traditional commitment to knowledge acquisition – typically gained through rigorous research and consideration of the evidence supporting a particular thesis or hypothesis – and a 21st century learning agenda featuring far less quantifiable skills and dispositions such as the 'four Cs': *communication, collaboration, creativity* and *critical thinking.* This tension is explored in a publication from the Australian Curriculum, Assessment and Reporting Authority (ACARA), the organisation responsible for the national curriculum.[3]

3   de Carvalho, D. (10 September 2022) ' 'Skills v knowledge' debate misses the crux of education,' *The Australian* https://www. acara.edu.au/news-and-media/acara-presentations/acara-ceo-article-september-2022

As much as the proponents of the 21st century learning agenda would have us believe it, the four Cs are not new to education. They are self-evident, quintessentially human skills and dispositions that have enabled extraordinary discovery and innovation over millennia. They are no more or less a product or necessity of human learning now than they were in any previous era. To assert otherwise is to fail to acknowledge the uniqueness and evolution of the human race.

Debating, which epitomises the human need and capacity to solve (and resolve) problems by way of verbal and written argument, belongs in the same category.

Ironically, 'critical thinking' gets such consistent attention from academics and policy makers around the world that one might conclude no previous generations ever considered it important.

In our view, globalist approaches attempt to make the case for replacing the tried and true with the experimental and unproven. We are already grappling with the consequences of decades of adopting numerous fads and trends without undertaking the due diligence necessary to determine their suitability in the Australian context.

As just one example, the unsubstantiated adoption of approaches to teaching English such as 'whole language', 'critical literacy', 'genre theory' and 'balanced literacy' has led to a decline in the linguistic competence and confidence of students and the professional preparation of teachers. This is particularly obvious in students' reading and writing skills, with one in five school leavers apparently unable to meet previous national minimum standards. These have been replaced with redeveloped standards that purport to set 'higher expectations'.[4]

4   Felton, K. (15 February 2023) 'New proficiency standards

Australian students' performance in national and international assessments reveals that too many lack competence in their national language compared to their peers in other systems, especially multilingual Singapore, where English is the language of instruction in most classrooms.

In 2023, the results of Australia's only national assessment program (NAPLAN) were not reassuring; about one in three students in Years 3, 5, 7 and 9 failed to reach minimum expectations in reading, writing and numeracy. The proportion of students performing at the highest levels is shrinking and the long tail of underachievers is growing.

Parents, employers, tertiary institutions and government reviews have all pointed to the lack of improvement in student achievement. A recent Productivity Commission report identified unsatisfactory educational outcomes.[5] We have written elsewhere about policy failure in education.[6]

for NAPLAN.' *Education Matters* https://www.educationmattersmag. com.au/new-proficiency-standards-for-naplan/

5 Australian Government. Productivity Commission. (December 2022) Review of the National School Reform Agreement (Study Report) https://www.pc.gov.au/inquiries/completed/school-agreement/report/school-agreement.pdf

6 See, for example, Clary, D. & Mueller, F. (28 July 2021) 'Writing matters: reversing a legacy of policy failure in Australian education', Centre for Independent Studies, Sydney https://www. cis.org.au/publication/writing-matters-reversing-a-legacy-of-policy-failure-in-australian-education

Mueller, F. (11 February 2021) 'A 2021 education resolution: keep an eye on the Australian Curriculum', Centre for Independent Studies, Sydney https://www.cis.org.au/publication/a-2021-education-resolution-keep-an-eye-on-the-australian-curriculum/

Mueller, F. & Donnelly, K. (2019) ' School Education Policy Paper', Page Research Centre, Canberra https://www.page.org.au/wp-content/uploads/2019/01/Page-Research-Centre-School-Education-Policy-Paper-2019-1.pdf

The risk for Australian education now is that subordinating human learning to technology – particularly through the use of artificial intelligence programs – will further dilute the requirement for original thought communicated in high quality English. Nationally consistent instruction and practice in debating could help to mitigate this risk. It would be an evidence-based approach to addressing multiple official education goals.

In past publications, we have pointed to Singapore's clear and consistent emphasis on both high-quality English (and other) language instruction and Character and Citizenship Education (CCE), which specifically aims to develop students' 'strong national identity'.[7]

Singapore's national curriculum claims to 'not leave learning to chance', explaining that:

CCE cannot be perceived in a silo or taught as a subject. Instead, the educational experience that we provide in our schools for our students needs to facilitate the coherent development of character and citizenship dispositions, and social-emotional well-being, across the total curriculum.

The Australian Curriculum's Civics and Citizenship material, which is tucked away inside the learning area of Humanities and Social Sciences, sets much less specific expectations for learning, places little emphasis on national identity and is not reflected 'across the total curriculum'.[8]

7   Singapore Ministry of Education. (2021) Student Development Curriculum Division - Character and Citizenship Education (Primary) Syllabus https://www.moe.gov.sg/-/media/files/syllabus/2021-primary-character-and-citizenship-education.ashx
8   ACARA. (2023) F-10 Australian Curriculum: Humanities and Social Sciences - Civics and Citizenship

The Civics and Citizenship curriculum aims to reinforce students' appreciation and understanding of what it means to be a citizen. It fosters responsible participation in Australia's democracy and explores ways in which students can actively shape their lives, value belonging to a diverse and dynamic society, and positively contribute locally, nationally, regionally and globally. As reflective, active and informed decision-makers, students will be well placed to contribute to an evolving and healthy democracy that fosters the wellbeing of Australia as a democratic nation.

Further, the design and delivery of Civics and Citizenship courses varies significantly across the country, particularly in Years 9 and 10 when 'students' access to Geography, Civics and Citizenship, and Economics and Business will be determined by school authorities or individual schools.'[9]

The near-invisible status of debating is seen, for example, in the Year 10 Civics and Citizenship curriculum, where that fundamental feature of a free and civil society – freedom of speech – gets just a brief mention.

This may involve students examining how our Western democratic heritage and values such as freedom of speech support participation in public debate about controversial issues; for example, the date of Australia Day, the Uluru Statement, reconciliation and truth-telling, or the call for a treaty between First Nations Australians and the Australian Government.

9   ACARA. (2023) Australian Curriculum - Humanities and Social Sciences (Version 9) https://v9.australiancurriculum.edu.au/teacher-resources/understand-this-learning-area/humanities-and-social-sciences

This suggestion appears under the Australian Curriculum's *Content elaborations*, which identify material that is not compulsory but may be used by teachers at their discretion. Notwithstanding the reference to 'public debate', there is no stated requirement for students to actually learn about, or practise, the traditional art of debating.

Yet in our modern Australian democracy, the place of debate is clear. It is explained in parliamentary guides such as Odgers' Australian Senate Practice.[10]

Debate fulfils one of the primary functions of the Senate, that of informing itself and the public by deliberation before decisions are made.

In Australia's lower house, debate is guided by House of Representatives Practice:[11]

Chapter 14 | Control and conduct of debate
The term 'debate' is a technical one meaning the argument for and against a question. In practice, the proceedings between a Member moving a motion (including the moving of the motion) [1] and the ascertainment by the Chair of the decision of the House constitute a debate. A decision may be reached without debate. In addition, many speeches by Members which are part of the normal routine of the House are excluded from the

10   Parliament of Australia. (2023) *Odgers' Australian Senate Practice, Chapter 10 - Debate.* https://www.aph.gov.au/About_Parliament/ Senate/Powers_practice_n_procedures/Odgers_Australian_Senate_ Practice/Chapter_10

11   Parliament of Australia. (2023) *House of Representatives Practice (7th Edition), Chapter 14 - Control and Conduct of Debate.* https://www. aph.gov.au/About_Parliament/House_of_Representatives/Powers_ practice_and_procedure/Practice7/HTML/Chapter14/Control_ and_conduct_of_debate

definition of debate, because there is no motion before the House. These include the asking and answering of questions, ministerial statements, matters of public importance, Members' statements and personal explanations. However, the word 'debate' is often used more loosely, to cover all words spoken by Members during House proceedings.

It is by debate that the House performs one of its more important roles, as emphasised by Redlich:

Without speech the various forms and institutions of parliamentary machinery are destitute of importance and meaning. Speech unites them into an organic whole and gives to parliamentary action self-consciousness and purpose. By speech and reply expression and reality are given to all the individualities and political forces brought by popular election into the representative assembly. Speaking alone can interpret and bring out the constitutional aims for which the activity of parliament is set in motion, whether they are those of the Government or those which are formed in the midst of the representative assembly. It is in the clash of speech upon speech that national aspirations and public opinion influence these aims, reinforce or counteract their strength. Whatever may be the constitutional and political powers of a parliament, government by means of a parliament is bound to trust to speech for its driving power, to use it as the main form of its action.[2]

The effectiveness of the debating process in Parliament has been seen as very much dependent on the principle of freedom of speech. Freedom of speech in the Parliament is guaranteed by the Constitution,[3] and derives ultimately from the United Kingdom Bill of Rights of 1688.[4] The privilege of freedom of speech was won by the British Parliament only after a long struggle to gain freedom of action from all influence of the Crown, courts of law and Government.

Logically, if debate (with all the specified constitutional implications for freedom of speech and assembly) remains a critical feature of Australian governance, it should be a key contributor to nurturing what the Alice Springs (Mparntwe) Declaration calls 'active and informed members of the community.'[12]

Students deserve to understand how debate has helped to get us to where we are in the Western world, and in Australia, in particular. Brave and determined people would not be silent when they had something important to say, arguing their case in public squares, town hall sessions, parliaments and other forums. Think about Australia's first Prime Minister, Edmund Barton, who developed his debating skills at the Sydney Mechanics' School of Arts, and the long-term Premier of New South Wales, Henry Parkes, who toured the country and engaged in countless wayside encounters with citizens in the lead-up to Federation in 1901. That is our history, and a free and civil society cannot afford to forget it.

It would be interesting to know whether students and their teachers discuss not simply the protocols of debating, but also the philosophical foundations of this skill, especially as part of the study of History and Civics and Citizenship.

How many teachers are intellectually and professionally grounded in these traditional practices that do, in fact, promote and develop the so-called 21st century skills of creativity, collaboration, critical thinking and communication?

12   Australian Government. Department of Education, Skills and Employment. (13 December 2019) The Alice Springs (Mparntwe) Declaration. https://www.education.gov.au/alice-springs-mparntwe-education-declaration

The art of debate (or argument) has its origins in ancient times, evolving and prized over centuries to become an intrinsic part of the culture of free nations and free people. For centuries, debating has served to enhance an individual's ability to structure and organise thoughts, constructing a sound argument on the basis of reason and evidence.

Socrates, Plato and Aristotle, among the best-known founders of Western education traditions, encouraged intellectual conversations – arguably, debates – about the greatest questions to which human beings can turn their minds.

At its best, a debate requires the speaker to convince an audience by exposing a weak case, a lack of substance and logic, and perhaps even factual errors. It assists participants to examine issues critically by detecting any gaps or errors in an opponent's arguments and counter-arguments. There is no room for opinion or feeling, only sound reasoning.

Socrates encouraged *reasoning* to expose truths about life, the overarching question being about how to live a better life. In this, speakers are interrogated about what they do know, all the while mindful that what they believe they know might not be true.

The Socratic approach to ethics was grounded in reason. Discussions about human virtues such as wisdom, justice, courage, and acts of piety and charity were the means of creating knowledge. Students interrogated their own beliefs, poised to learn from their ignorance, confusion or error, rather than simply regurgitating the ideas and interpretations of others.

At the heart of reasoning is the necessity to think for oneself, to question one's own thinking, and not to look for quick or simplistic answers. The process requires building on prior knowledge as new understanding develops.

In more recent times, American philosopher and educational theorist John Dewey described the act of the scholar 'turning a subject over in the psyche, giving it genuine and back-to-back consideration.'[13] Dewey believed in the 'social intelligence' of human beings, reflected in their capacity to solve problems collaboratively, as a critical factor in improving society.

Nelson Mandela, lawyer, civil rights activist and South Africa's first democratically elected President, saw debate as a means of achieving genuine collaboration.[14]

A good leader can engage in a debate frankly and thoroughly, knowing that at the end he and the other side must be closer, and thus emerge stronger. You don't have that idea when you are arrogant, superficial and uninformed.

Collaboration, as mentioned earlier, is one of the designated 21st century skills.

Online learning seemingly works against any revival of debating in the traditional sense. However, variations on online discussion including forums, break-out groups and chat platforms have been successfully integrated into educational programs, especially for older students, with an emphasis on collaboration. Expert guidance from teachers of all subjects, underpinned by rigorous research, can ensure students learn from and with each other, as opposed to simply alongside each other.

13   Dewey, J. (1910) *How we think?* Lexington, Mass: D.C. Heath, 1-13
14   Nelson Mandela Foundation. (2023) https://www. nelsonmandela.org/news/entry/nelson-mandela-foundation-responds-to-alleged-comments-from-president-trump-on-nelson-mandela

It is difficult to quantify the commitment to debating in Australian schools. According to the Australian Debating Federation, about 30,000 Australian students participate in debating competitions each year.[15] The ADF says that:

> *Debating training imparts lifelong skills to students, including confidence in speaking in public to peers, an ability to logically make and assess arguments, and a willingness to engage with, and learn from, those with different opinions.*

These students, and their coaches and supporters, stand out from mainstream education.

The Australian Curriculum developed for students in Foundation to Year 10 offers a continuum of learning in eight learning areas, seven General Capabilities and three Cross-Curriculum Priorities.

Depending on the interests and decisions of their teachers, the Australian Curriculum's English programs for Foundation to Year 10 'may involve students' in debating.

That there are at least a few references scattered across its various dimensions indicates that the Australian Curriculum acknowledges, albeit to a very limited degree, the contribution that debating can make to teaching and learning.

However, there is no overarching advice to help students in F-10 and their teachers understand the origins and benefits of debating. The increased attention paid to debating in the senior secondary curriculum emphasises the disconnect between the minimal focus on that skill during the earlier years of schooling and what is expected of students later in Years 11 and 12.

---

15   The Australian Debating Federation (2023) https://www. debating.org.au/

The seven General Capabilities reflect the 21st century learning agenda, identifying skills and attributes allegedly essential for students in the new millennium.

- Critical and Creative Thinking
- Ethical Understanding
- Intercultural Understanding
- Literacy
- Numeracy
- Personal and Social Capability
- Digital Literacy (previously Information and Communication Technology)

Critical and Creative Thinking is designed around four elements (Inquiring, Generating, Analysing and Reflecting) and would seem a logical place for a focus on debating. However, none of the Capabilities make a clear place for it in their continua of learning.

The Cross-Curriculum Priorities are:

- Aboriginal and Torres Strait Islander Histories and Cultures
- Asia and Australia's Engagement with Asia
- Sustainability

As with the General Capabilities, the CCPs specify no place for debating.

Although the Australian Curriculum also sets expectations for senior secondary subjects, we emphasise that each Australian state and territory makes its own arrangements regarding curriculum, assessment and qualifications for students in Years 11 and 12.

A key word search for 'debate' in the Australian Curriculum for senior secondary students reveals some three dozen references. The majority of references are in the *Content descriptions,* which mandate material for study.

A survey of English, Mathematics, the Sciences and Humanities and the Social Sciences (HASS) shows no consistency about how debate might be incorporated in teaching across senior secondary learning areas.

In English and Geography, for example, these older students are encouraged to practise the art of debating. In the Sciences, students explore ways in which a field of knowledge contributes to contemporary debate, but there is no requirement to actually practise debating. The Modern History curriculum challenges students to examine and interpret significant ideas and events of the 20th century, focusing on how these fuelled political debate, but they are not invited to test their own interpretations through active debate.

CONCLUSION

As older teenagers begin to think about post-school life and work, they are also approaching voting age. The journey into adulthood – especially in a free and civil society – involves developing the skills to take a position on a range of issues and to make the case effectively.

Technological advances are exerting enormous pressure on countries to develop more and new skills in the workforce, and Australia must find innovative ways to help its youngest citizens prepare for the future. At the same time, longstanding skills consistent with Australia's national heritage and the Western traditions, values and way of life characteristic of a free and civil society, must be preserved. The art of debating is one such skill.

Given that the rationale for introducing a national curriculum is 'to improve the quality, equity and transparency of Australia's education system', we believe that all three goals would be well served by prioritising debating across the whole curriculum. This would ensure greater consistency in students' study of English and other learning areas from Foundation to Year 12, reinforcement of critical thinking and communication skills, and clarity for teachers, parents and other stakeholders.

THE INCOHERENCE OF BABEL
Kenneth Crowther

ABSTRACT

There is a deep incoherence at the heart of the modern west. Not only should it be plain for all to see, but when seen, it has the power to reveal the emptiness and confusion of many contemporary social and political movements. This paper contends that exposing this incoherence is a vital step often missed in cultural debate. The modern Tower of Babel is built on shoddy foundations; when these foundations are exposed, perhaps the tower might fall. But this approach requires much of us. Firstly, our own foundations must be strong, and our own worldviews must be coherent. Secondly, we must strengthen the foundations of the next generation, because incoherence is inconsequential to the poorly educated.

In the third chapter of *Orthodoxy*, G.K. Chesterton provides one his quintessentially prophetic quotes; its prescience speaks not only to his time, but to ours as well. With his typical wit, he dissects the growing scepticism of the age due to what he calls the suicide of thought - a way of thinking that cancels out all other thinking:

> *...the new rebel is a sceptic, and will not entirely trust anything. He has no loyalty; therefore, he can never be really a revolutionist. And the fact that he doubts everything really gets in his way when he wants to denounce anything. For all denunciation implies a moral doctrine of some kind; and the modern revolutionist doubts not only the institution he denounces, but the doctrine by*

which he denounces it… As a politician, he will cry out that war is a waste of life, and then, as a philosopher, that all life is waste of time. A Russian pessimist will denounce a policeman for killing a peasant, and then prove by the highest philosophical principles that the peasant ought to have killed himself… The man of this school goes first to a political meeting, where he complains that savages are treated as if they were beasts; then he takes his hat and umbrella and goes on to a scientific meeting, where he proves that they practically are beasts… In his book on politics he attacks men for trampling on morality; in his book on ethics he attacks morality for trampling on men. Therefore the modern man in revolt has become practically useless for all purposes of revolt. By rebelling against everything he has lost his right to rebel against anything.[16]

Such is Chesterton's insight that this passage applies equally today to the topic of this book: the woke movement. There is a deep incoherence at the heart of wokery, a dismantling and deconstructing anti-authoritarian, anti-essentialist approach to reality that, as Chesterton says, 'undermin[es] its own mines'[17]. It is the contention of this paper that this incoherence presents one of the keys to combatting the movement, but only if we are not participants in incoherence ourselves.

As always, we must begin with definitions. But before I can, I must admit that 'woke' is not a word I like to use very often. I think its connotations are too complicated, and it holds a series of connections and allegiances that often do damage to the causes of those who invoke it. The word is almost exclusively used by people against it - as a pejorative.

16   Chesterton, G.K., *Orthodoxy*, (Chicago: Moody Publishers, 2009), pp.65-66.
17   Ibid., p.66.

The woke themselves rarely use it; rather, they talk about being inclusive, caring, empathetic, self-aware, and anti-racist. And I think that for a large amount of them it is an authentic desire that comes from a noble place - a point I will return to later.

So how should we define this word? In many ways it operates as a placeholder for a raft of socially progressive ideas and policies that are rejected by many on the broadly defined right, but more specifically conservatives and perhaps some liberals. The reasons for this rejection are not single-faceted. Some reject it because it is often anti-liberal, such as compelling speech: this is what initially shot Jordan Peterson into fame - his rejection of Bill C-16 in Canada that compelled certain speech with regards to gender pronouns. Others reject this so-called social progress because they see it as a thinly veiled reimagining of Marxism, and they are historically aware enough to know that this ideology has literally never ended well. There are others again who reject what they call the woke movement because they can see the damage it is doing, particularly to young people. And then there are others who suggest it is ultimately anti-humanist and perhaps even anti-Christ. These are all fine reasons for rejecting wokery. I would still suggest, however, that they are not necessarily fine reasons for using the word, because throwing it around is like a red rag to a bull. If you are trying to get a reaction - go right ahead. But getting emotional reactions is not the same as presenting winning, compelling, and winsome arguments. It is far easier, and far less effective.

While I generally accept all the above variations of the definition, I want to add to it a broader definition that speaks to its foundations. I want to propose that at the heart of the woke movement is a self-sabotaging suicide of thought, but not only of thought, but also of reason and communication - of coherence itself. This is why I have entitled this paper The Incoherence of Babel, because incoherence forms the foundation of the woke movement. This incoherence is now becoming so obvious that it can no longer be ignored, though I believe it has a long heritage, and understanding this heritage is fundamental to knowing what to do about it.

You may be familiar with the story of Babel that comes from Genesis 11. Humanity comes together to build a tower to reach to Heaven, and it ends with their language being confused. C.S. Lewis employs this imagery in the dystopian vision of *That Hideous Strength*, the much under-read third book of the *Ransom Trilogy*. In it, a group of progressives calling themselves the National Institute of Coordinated Experiments, or the N.I.C.E., attempt to bring about a new order of humanity. At the risk of spoilers for those who have not read it, one of the results of this Babel-like attempt is that their language becomes confused and they are subjected to the violent chaos that results from incoherent babble.

The goal of the N.I.C.E. is to become the new gods of a new world. There is at one point a brilliant summation of the processes at work in their minds:

Despair of objective truth had been increasingly insinuated into the scientists' indifference to it, and a concentration upon power had been the result... Dreams of the far future destiny of man were dragging up from its shallow and unquiet grave the old dream of Man as God... What should they find incredible, since they believed no longer in a rational universe? What should they regard as too obscene, since they held that all morality was a mere subjective by-product of the physical and economic situations of men? ... There was now at last a real chance for

31

fallen Man to shake off that limitation of his powers which mercy had imposed upon him as a protection from the full results of his fall. If this succeeded, hell would be at last incarnate.[18]

Lewis, like Chesterton, is prophetic. The clues to the babble of wokery are all in this passage: despair of objective truth; concentration upon power; the old dream of Man as God; the impossibility of obscenity in the moral vacuum of a purely subjective world. And indeed, in our own world, are not every day new obscenities being codified, academicized, dressed-up in media-spin and then accepted not only as not obscene, but actually held up as beautiful and good?

The result and the price of these animating desires is incoherence. But this also provides the key to recognising the problem, the key to disarming it, and the key to responding to it. Focusing on coherence helps to clarify exactly what has been undermined in the modern west. If we focus on the issues, not the individuals, we can have some modicum of success; however, this is like putting out spot fires with our shoes while a bushfire ravages the land. We must attack it at first principles, because at first principles, wokery fails miserably.

Perhaps it is now incumbent on me to prove that the woke movement is, in fact, incoherent. I will do so by attempting to reimagine the Chesterton passage quoted earlier, adapting it for the year 2023:

The new intellectual is woke, and will only trust his feelings. He has no loyalty; therefore, he can never enjoy real community. And the fact that he doubts everything would reveal his inconsistency if anyone thought consistently. As a politician in one chamber he will cry we must save the

18   Lewis, C.S., *That Hideous Strength*, (New York: Scribner, 2003), pp.200-201.

environment for future generations, and in another he'll legislate the destruction of those generations before they're born. As a female CEO she'll praise the advantages of a boardroom with more women than men, and then as an enlightened progressive she'll suggest that women basically are men. As a firm supporter of women's professional sporting teams, he'll fight for those teams to be filled with biological males. As a state party leader, he'll advocate for women's rights while ejecting women from his party who advocate for women's existence. On his twitter account he'll celebrate modern sexual freedom so that people can date whoever they're physically attracted to, before piling on comments attacking a previous ally as transphobic because they're not physically attracted to a trans person. The modern universities believe their job is to listen to students rather than for students to listen to them, and in the name of learning they cancel anyone from whom they might learn. Therefore, the modern man obsessed with deconstruction has become practically useless for all purposes of constructive conversation. By asserting the incoherence of everything, he has become incoherent to everyone, even himself.

Like Chesterton's sceptic and Lewis' N.I.C.E., woke incoherence emerges from a hatred of limitations. In the pursuit of freedom, humanity follows a spiralling tendency to reject the limitations of being human: those tyrannies of biology, of sexual reproduction, of the family - in short, the tyranny of reality. It is argued that for the sake of progress, this tyranny must be rejected. We must assert our power to redefine reality as we see fit, because if there is any kind of objective reality that we did not determine, then we are not in control. Objective order necessarily comes from outside of ourselves. That we are created beings subject to a creator within a created order is the greatest of heresies for the orthodox progressive. Created order must be rejected, but the cost of this rejection is the loss of order itself, hence the slide into incoherence.

Order is logical, coherent, and meaningful. Each of these words could be subsumed into an ancient concept that has its roots in Greek philosophy and the fathers of the Christian church; a concept upon which western civilisation was built, and the rejection of which is the reason for its collapse: the logos.

Peter Kreeft, a professor of philosophy at Boston College, has explained the breadth of meaning that this term encompasses. In his series of lectures on *The Platonic Tradition*, he defines the logos as 'the ultimate truth about the nature of all things.'[19] He then proposes a tripartite way of thinking about logos: that there are three forms of logos that all equally represent the fullness of its meaning. While the word has dozens of meanings, they all fit under three headings: metaphysical, psychological, and linguistic. Firstly, the metaphysical realm of logos includes definitions like realness, order, truth, and meaning. The second umbrella-term of psychological includes words like wisdom, understanding, reason, and logic. This is, as he explains, the 'human psychological internalisation of the first logos, the metaphysical logos.'[20] The third part then is the communicative or spoken externalisation of the psychological; this is the linguistic, and its definitions include words, language, speech, communication, and explanation. There is a clear connection between these three logoi. As he says, 'Logos number three is a mind's externalisation of logos number two, as logos number

19   Kreeft, Peter. *Christian Platonism*, www.youtube.com/watch?v=3sfjlZEpU0o
20   Ibid.

two is a mind's internalisation of logos number one.'[21] The linguistic is the mind's externalisation of the psychological, which is the mind's internalisation of the metaphysical.

Kreeft then goes on to explain that the whole history of philosophy has been structured around the dismissal and denial of these three realities:

> *Premodern philosophy - ancient and medieval - centred on metaphysics and ended with the nominalism of William of Ockham, which was a denial of logos number one - intelligible universals. Then classical modern philosophy, beginning with Descartes and Bacon, centred on epistemology, and ended in the empiricist scepticism of Hume and the even more radical scepticism of Kant, who denied that anyone could ever know things as they are in themselves; in other words, objective reality... Finally, twentieth-century philosophy concentrated on philosophy of language and culminated in deconstructionism, which is the denial of logos number three, the denial that words can tell truths.[22]*

This, according to Kreeft, is the history of philosophy - the gradual denial of logos, which of course has coincided with the gradual denial of the reality of Christ and with it the denial of any kind of reality at all. Kreeft explains that our world is shaped by these three ideas: 'First, there is no intelligible reality, no order and meaning to reality. Second, even if there were, it could never be known, never understood. Third, even if anyone did understand it, it could never be communicated.'[23]

21   Ibid.
22   Ibid.
23   Ibid.

35

While it has lurked in the shadows of academia for the last few decades, the linguistic denial has now become obvious and undeniable. We have pulled apart words, and meaning itself is beginning to fray. This is in part the result of a process of deconstruction propelled by members of the Frankfurt school and later postmodern figures such as Michel Foucault. Discussion about the Marxist foundations of woke ideas is important and needed, and I am in no way criticising this approach. However, this alone is not enough. Unfortunately, it is simply not sufficient to point out logically, cohesively, and coherently where the origins of the radical left lie, and what damage these ideologies have done over time. While these efforts do have significant impact, they alone are insufficient because logical, cohesive, and coherent arguments are like water off a duck's back to those that have swallowed the linguistic logos denial. You have perhaps wondered at this yourself - how people seem to be so recalcitrant in the face of clear and articulate logic. It is because they no longer believe in it.

The incoherence of Babel relies upon the denial of meaning, which rests upon the denial of order. When Friedrich Nietzsche wrote of the madman proclaiming the death of God, he was right to say that his time had not yet come, because the people surrounding him had not grappled with the gravity of the implications of murdering God. God had been slowly dying since the unintended revolutions of the metaphysical and psychological denials. Nietzsche knew that his society was living on borrowed time. He knew that meaning had died, while those around him still held on to the vestiges of meaning and purpose that only come from submitting to created order. It was not until that final denial, the relatively recent death of communication itself - what we might call to use Roland Barthes' words, *The Death of the Author* - that the impact of those other two deaths - the metaphysical and the psychological - has started to be felt. This is what we are feeling now.

Wokery is predicated upon the denial of logocentrism. In this it is certainly built upon the work of the Frankfurt School and the cultural Marxism that emerged from that movement. Nevertheless, we should be careful with our language when invoking the shadow of these ideas to explain the woke movement. We cannot commit logical fallacies and must be careful to avoid strawmen. While the looming figure of Marx is certainly responsible for elements of cultural Marxism, he himself was *not* a 'cultural Marxist', and quite likely would have disavowed the movement. It also must be recognised that most of today's so-called cultural Marxists, certainly most of those under forty years old (who tend to be the loudest), have not read Marx. The average woke militant today is an accidental Marxist. What is known is that feelings, not facts, are sovereign, and that oppression is bad. Rather than foisting definitions upon others, which they can honestly ignorantly deny, we should take them seriously when they define themselves.

In the name of doing just that, I offer a definition of woke by a man named Adam Vasco who describes his occupation as a Director of Diversity & Inclusion in Professional Practice. This is a definition that I believe we must take seriously. On 24 May 2023, Vasco posted the following on his LinkedIn account:

> *There's a phenomenon afoot in the social discourse, a peculiar inversion of language where the term 'woke' has been repurposed as an insult. It is a pointed dart flung with derision, meant to stigmatise those committed to awareness, understanding, and activism around social issues such as racism, inequality, and*

injustice. And yet, when faced with this misguided weaponisation of language, I suggest we embrace it. Smile, and simply say 'thank you'.

…the word has been co-opted and leveraged as a pejorative, a signal to marginalise and ridicule those who believe in the necessity of societal change. The term 'woke' is brandished like an emblem of shame, a scarlet letter for the socially conscious.

Consider this, however: if being 'woke' means standing up against bigotry, advocating for equality, challenging ingrained societal norms that perpetuate injustice, then we should not only accept this label but wear it with pride…

Critics would say that being 'woke' is a form of virtue signaling [sic], a way of projecting moral superiority without the need for substantive action. They may argue that it's a superficial gloss on deep-seated and complex issues. But in the face of such criticism, it's important to remember that awareness is the first step toward change. Recognising and naming a problem is a crucial part of the process of addressing it…

Being 'woke' is not about being, self-righteous, or divisive. It's about being conscious, compassionate, and committed to change. Embrace it, champion it, and use it as a tool for awareness, understanding, and activism.[24]

I must admit that if this is what woke means, if it is what it really means, and if it means only this and nothing more than this, then I really don't have a problem with it. On this definition, some of my heroes are woke. William Wilberforce, St Thomas More, Martin Luther King Jr, even Jesus himself was woke under this definition. As Vasco says, 'If being 'woke' means standing up against bigotry, advocating for equality, challenging ingrained societal norms that perpetuate injustice, then we should not only accept this label but wear

24   Vasco, Adam. *LinkedIn*, 24 May 2023.

it with pride.' I could not agree more. However, perhaps before doing so, it might be prudent to ask some important questions of definition: what exactly does 'bigotry' mean? What about 'equality', or 'injustice'?

It is not 'standing up against injustice' that we disagree about. I too believe in standing up against injustice. The disagreement is about the definition of words. And this is why understanding the denial of the logos is so important when considering how to deal with the negative elements of the woke movement. More than ever, words have slippery meanings; consider all the recent examples of elected officials and judges struggling to define what a woman is. So, this is the first place that I might end up disagreeing with Vasco - the definition of words. And then after that comes the just as important question of what steps are justifiable to take in the process of standing up against injustice. In the wise words of the namesake of this book's publication, Christopher Dawson, 'As soon as men decide that all means are permitted to fight an evil, then their good becomes indistinguishable from the evil that they set out to destroy.'[25] This accurately summarises the dissonance underpinning the woke movement. In the name of tolerance, they become intolerant. In the name of freedom, they supress freedoms. In the name of some human rights, they eradicate others.

Despite Vasco's claims that it is not mere virtue signalling or 'a way of projecting moral superiority without the need for substantive action', being woke often becomes exactly that. The sheer volume of conflict surrounding it suggests that Vasco is wrong when he says that being woke 'is not about being, self-righteous, or divisive,' because conflict is always two-sided. Unfortunately, but unsurprisingly, what wokery so

25   Dawson, Christoper. *The Judgement of the Nations*, (Washington DC: The Catholic University of America Press, 2011), pp.9-10.

easily becomes is the desire to be seen as caring. The desire to be seen often outstrips the actual care by magnitudes. How do we know this? Because none of our political parties except perhaps for the Greens, and probably not even them, are truly wedded to the kind of Marxist concern for power imbalances that have shaped the political culture they have inherited. And this is for a simple reason: they are the power. It is very difficult for powerful people to be properly Marxist in the genuine sense, because as soon as they gain the power to make the change, they become the problem. Virtue signalling concern for people therefore becomes the most important element because it takes the focus away from the fact that the virtue signaller has, in fact, amassed for themselves significant power. Powerless people are not interested in signalling, they are too busy trying to survive.

If the question for the papers collected in this book is how to respond to the woke movement, it is in some ways a question of what should be asserted in its place. My answer is it cannot simply be to rewind the clock to some recent illusory golden age. We did not start to go wrong just due to the postmodern turn. This is not just a problem of Marxism, not even of the 20th Century. What is required is a return to reality: a full return to logocentrism. We must not replace the incoherence of wokery with some other form of incoherence. It is vital that those who combat the woke movement today ensure they are not unconsciously saying, 'We do not like this particular incoherence - not because it is incoherent, but simply because we are not in control of it!' How close we ourselves come to entertaining the power dynamics of Marxism if it turns out we only get upset when our control and power is threatened. We cannot believe truth and goodness are on our sides if we only reject that which we so happen not to like.

What then is a solution? I have suggested here that not just wokery, but that modernity itself, is predicated upon the denial of the logos. I have also made the claim that incoherence is not a persuasive argument for people who do not believe that coherence is even possible. Logic, rationality, and common sense will not win the day if the day does not care for these things. How can we combat the intolerance of people who truly believe they're fighting for tolerance? In the words of one of Aleksandr Solzhenitsyn's characters: 'It's a universal law - intolerance is the first sign of an inadequate education. An ill-educated person behaves with arrogant impatience, whereas truly profound education breeds humility.'[26] Humility: this must be part of the character of the solution.

If it is not the entire answer, education is at least a large portion of it. Education is where the rejection of the linguistic logos has taken root, which is why the loudest, proudest, most combative, but also the most well-intentioned and unaware of the woke are often young and educated. The forty-year process of ceding power and influence in the education sector was one of the most damaging and foolish things that those on the side of the logos could ever have done. But it is not a lost cause. The beauty of education is that it gets a fresh start every year. It starts with children, and despite what we are told, children naturally believe in reality. We are naturally logocentric beings and need to be taught, need in fact to be indoctrinated, that reality is not real. Nature is on the side of reality, and reality is on the side of the logos. Every young child first learning to speak and read presents the possibility of a return to sanity, meaning, and purpose.

26 Solzhenitsyn, Aleksandr, *August 1914*, (London: Penguin Books, 1974), p.428.

We must teach coherence. Real education, which best emerges from a traditional classical approach to the liberal arts, reveals the sham that lies at the heart of the woke movement. To put the situation as bluntly as possible, Christian schools, of all denominations, are failing at this. They are not necessarily failing at producing acceptably well-adjusted citizens who have a modicum of faith or at least interest in Jesus. But not only is this not enough, but these are things that should rest primarily with the family and the Church, not the school. The school's task is to teach students how to think and speak well and to inculcate wisdom and virtue; this means bringing them into harmony with the metaphysical, the psychological, and the linguistic by teaching the reality of the logos.

This kind of education, often called classical education, is not predicated primarily on being anti-woke. It is not even interested terms like this; they didn't exist for most of human history. However, it will by default address the woke issue, as young people are taught to seek the good, the true, and the beautiful, to seek the logos, and then to communicate about it effectively. In 2023, classical education is a small but growing movement in Australia.

A currently proposed new school in Brisbane, intending to open in 2026, is named after St John Henry Newman. His vision of education addresses these issues without needing to throw stones or build straw men, without invoking Marx or wokery. This kind of education:

> ...*gives a man a clear, conscious view of their own opinions and judgements, a truth in developing them, an eloquence in expressing them, and a force in urging them. It teaches him to see things as they are, to go right to the point, to disentangle a*

skein of thought to detect what is sophistical and to discard what is irrelevant.[27]

This education - classical education - is a remedy for the incoherence of Babel.

27   Newman, John Henry. *The Idea of a University*, (London: Basil Montague Pickering, 1873), p.178.

LOOKING BACKWARD LEADS US FORWARD: THE TRUE NATURE OF CONSERVATISM

Kevin Donnelly

ABSTRACT

One of the tropes used by the cultural-left when denigrating conservatism is to attack it as backward looking, ossified and irrelevant. At the same time, neo-Marxist inspired activists argue the history of Western civilisation is riven with injustice, oppression and violence against what Edward Said describes as the 'other'.

The reality, instead of being backward looking and ossified, is that conservatism acknowledges the need to re-evaluate what we have inherited and to appreciate, where necessary, the need for change. In addition to culture involving 'the best which has been thought and said in the world' Matthew Arnold also argues it is important to turn 'a fresh and free thought upon our stock notions and habits'. T S Eliot makes a similar point when arguing the need is 'to maintain the continuity of our culture – and neither continuity, nor respect for the past, implies standing still'.

It's ironic, while the indigenous welcome to country asks everyone to acknowledge and value 'traditional custodians' and 'elders past and present', the same respect is not given to the heritage and elders associated with Western civilisation.

Augusto del Noce observes:

> *Doctrinally, conservatism is reached through a critique of utopia, of the idea that it is possible to achieve worldly situations in which all contradictions have been solved, and to create conditions in which there is a perfect harmony between virtue and happiness, so that happiness can be realized without effort and without sacrifice.*[28]

One of the arguments used against conservatism by cultural-left critics is to attack it as backward looking, ossified and irrelevant. Critics argue there is nothing to be learned or valued from the past and that the school curriculum, for example, must be forward looking, flexible and dynamic.[29] Only by adopting 21st century learning will students, in the much loved clichés employed by new-age educators, become creative, adaptive, life-long learners capable of coping with an uncertain and ever-changing future.

At the same time as prioritising a future's approach to learning, cultural-left critics argue the history of Western civilisation is riven with injustice, oppression and violence against what Edward Said describes as the 'other'.[30] Such is the strength of this antagonism that academics at the University of Sydney opposed accepting money from the Ramsay Centre for Western Civilisation, supposedly, as any

---

28   Augusto Del Noce. *The Crisis Of Modernity*. Translated by Carlo Lancellotti. Canada. McGill-Queen's University Press. 2014. P.54

29   For an example of how 21st century learning dominates schools see the *21st Century Education!* video available on the Australian Institute for Teaching and School Leadership website, https://www.aitsl.edu.au/tools-resources/resource/21st-century-education Accessed 17 July 2023.

30   Edward Said. *Orientalism*. New York. Pantheon Books.

centre established would be guilty enforcing a 'conservative, culturally essentialist and Eurocentric approach'.[31]

The reality, instead of being backward looking and ossified, is that conservatism acknowledges the need to re-evaluate what is passed from one generation to the next. Edmund Burke, who many consider the father of conservatism and who wrote at the time of the French Revolution, argues 'A state without the means of change is without the means of its conservation'.[32] While acknowledging and respecting what he terms 'a patrimony derived from our forefathers,'[33] Burke argues it is important to accept what he terms 'a principle of improvement'.[34]

The key difference, though, between how Burke defines change and the type of change represented by the French Revolution is that while one is nihilistic and destructive of past institutions and way of life, the other is based on the need for caution and temperateness. In opposition to events in France that led to Madame Guillotine and the reign of terror, Burke cites the strengths and benefits of the Westminster parliamentary system and British common law. A system that evolved over hundreds of years since the time of the Magna Carta, the Glorious Revolution and the various Reform Acts that restricted the power of the monarchy, made the electoral system less corrupt and led to more citizens being able to vote.

That conservatism is not unchanging and static is also proven by Matthew Arnold's admonition, while culture

31   Open letter from University of Sydney academics – No to collaboration between the Ramsay Centre for Western Civilisation and the University. http://ramsayoffcampus.org/open-letter/ Accessed 17 July 2023.
32   Edmund Burke. *Reflections on the Revolution in France*. New York. Oxford University Press. P.21.
33   Ibid. P.32.
34   Ibid. P.33.

involves becoming familiar with 'the best that has been thought and said in the world',[35] equally as important is turning 'a stream of fresh and free thought upon our stock notions and habits which we follow staunchly but mechanically'.[36] Once again, similar to Burke, the belief is the process of enculturation does not happen intuitively or by accident. In order for society to prosper and flourish it is vital to view it as what Burke describes as a contract involving 'a partnership not only between those who are living, but between those who are dead, and those who are yet to be born'.[37] At the same time, unlike totalitarian regimes that seek to return to year zero on the basis society's institutions and way of life must be destroyed if the revolution is to succeed, Burke advocates scepticism about unwarranted and unjustified change.

A third defender of conservatism who acknowledges the need for change as well as continuity is the British philosopher, Michael Oakeshott. In his essay 'On being conservative'[38] Oakeshott writes instead of idolising 'what is past and gone,'[39] the emphasis should be on valuing and appreciating those aspects of the past that have something purposeful and significant to offer those living in the present. While accepting the need for change Oakeshott, similar to Burke, also warns against revolutionary change given its violent and disruptive nature.

In associating conservatism with a particular disposition, Oakeshott differentiates between change and innovation. While the first, for example when the seasons change, is to

---

35   Matthew Arnold. *Culture and Anarchy*. London. Cambridge University Press. P.6
36   Ibid. P.6.
37   Edmund Burke. Op. cit. P.96.
38   Michael Oakeshott. 'On being 'conservative' in *Rationalism in politics and other essays*. Indianapolis. Liberty Press. PP.407-437.
39   Ibid. P.408.

be accommodated, the second, as it involves human agency and design, requires caution. Oakeshott warns 'there is no such things as unqualified improvement'.[40] Innovation, to be warranted, needs to beneficial, not lead to undesirable or unforeseen consequences, address a specific issue or problem and not be undertaken too rapidly so as to allow time to evaluate its impact and effectiveness.

It's obvious the climate activists and governments replacing coal and gas with solar and wind power have never read Oakeshott. Such is the harmful impact of such change that while the wealthy and privileged can deal with the rising cost of living and keeping warm in winter, society's most vulnerable suffer poverty and deprivation.

A second example of the dangers of change driven by radical ideology instead of rationality and common sense involves the neo-Marxist inspired gender and sexuality Safe Schools program. The program indoctrinates primary and secondary age students with the belief boys can be girls and girls can be boys. Instead of being God-ordained and a biological reality, being male or female is defined as a social construct imposed by a binary, heteronormative, capitalist society.

According to Roz Ward, one of the designers of the program, Safe Schools was designed to herald a neo-Marxist inspired utopia where human 'sexuality, gender and how we relate to our bodies can blossom in new and amazing ways that we can only try to imagine today'.[41] Proven by the closure of the British gender-transitioning clinic Tavistock and the over 1000 families taking action to sue the clinic for medical negligence, it's obvious what Ward hoped for has not, and will not, eventuate.

40   Ibid. P.411.
41   Roz Ward. Marxism 2106 Conference. https://www.youtube.com/watch?v=0mMOfOdRE0M Accessed 25 July 2023.

The conservative Italian philosopher and social critic Augusto Del Noce, similar to Burke and Oakeshott, also accepts societies evolve and change over time. Del Noce, illustrated by the rise of fascism and communism, warns against revolutionary change based on the mistaken belief a worldly utopia can be achieved by erasing the past and destroying existing institutions.

Del Noce suggests the fact particular institutions have existed for some time suggests, not-withstanding the need for improvement, they are beneficial. Del Noce writes conservatives accept the 'general principle that the duration of a given country's institutions proves that they exist for a reason, and that modifications and improvements are possible, but always within the context of such institutions'.[42] It should be noted that Edmund Burke in *Reflections on the Revolution in France* puts the same argument.

As previously mentioned, while those responsible for the French Revolution destroyed existing institutions and were responsible for the reign of terror, it was the gradual evolution of existing British institutions that eventually led to popular sovereignty and a common law system protecting citizen's rights and freedoms. It was also the British parliament that abolished slavery throughout the empire while the practice continued elsewhere around the globe.

POSTSCRIPT

It is ironic that many of those critical of acknowledging and valuing Western civilisation's patrimony on the basis there is little of value in looking to the past as society must be forward looking are so keen to promote Indigenous history. Across

---

42   Augusto Del Noce. *The Crisis Of Modernity.* Translated by Carlo Lancellotti. Canada. McGill-Queen's University Press. 2014.

the nation 'Welcome to country' has become mandatory as citizens, young and old, are told to acknowledge the 'traditional custodians' and 'elders past and present'. The desire to laud, at the time of the arrival of First Fleet's landing in 1788, what Karl Popper describes as a 'tribal or closed society',[43] also suggests a degree of historical amnesia.

43   Karl Popper. *The Open Society and Its Enemies*. Oxford. Routledge Classics. P.XXXV.

ESSAYS FOR AUSTRALIA
Sarah Flynn-O'Dea

ABSTRACT

Western society has undergone an inexorable shift in how we perceive reality. Increasingly, the emphasis is on shaping reality to our will. However, historically, the accurate perception of reality 'as it is' was considered the skill of a wiseman. Thus, it could be argued, we have turned our back on wisdom. This presentation will delve into causes and associated consequences of modern worldview, and its associated 'negative thinking' and 'critical theory' paradigms, with a focus on its impacts in education. I will discuss some of the genealogy and mechanics of woke academia, highlighting the work of Author James Lindsay of the 'Grievance Studies' fame and some personal experiences as a 'woke' graduate of the 90's. Additionally, I will outline the principles of Classical Education and argue for its key role in dismantling woke ideology using the popular psychological paradigm of the wellbeing/ human flourishing movement.

INTRODUCTION

If politics is downstream of culture, then culture is certainly downstream of education. As we look to the fast approaching national referendum on the Voice, and the polarised, emotion-driven and anti-intellectual debate that has surrounded it, the depressing trend in the standard of discourse in this country is an indictment on an education system that has settled for ideology over true intellectual cultivation. So what are the mechanisms by which this erosion of intellectual skill have been accomplished and what are we to do about it?

As a teacher, mother and thinker I have spent the past decade or so on a self-guided journey of educational recovery from reading 'all the wrong books' to experiencing a great sense of relief and hope for the future of our country in the world of great books, great ideas and the proposition of educational renewal via Classical education in the Liberal Arts tradition.

As a young person, I was positioned to ostensibly receive the best education possible. I had 12 years of Catholic education, my secondary in a high-end inner city girls' school in Brisbane. However, I left school knowing nothing about the big answers in life. This is what I craved and so I did what many young Brisbane x-gen searching for answers did, I went to the University of Queensland. I studied ecology in Bachelor of Science and Bachelor of Arts in Geography and French. After becoming suitably captured by activist notions of social justice, I did the only right thing and moved my major into Aboriginal and Torres Strait Islander studies unit. In all sincerity, I had a deep love of this country, the land and its first people. However, the activist influence in this unit resulted not in a development of this passion, an empowerment or partnership, but a learning how to loathe myself and every aspect of my culture.

The same was echoed loudly in ecology studies where the resounding message, was not the awe of nature but the condemnation of humanity and the overarching narrative of its wholesale exploitation of nature and interminable trajectory toward mass extinction. Whilst obviously human impacts and over-exploitation of natural resources should be subject to responsible stewardship, the condemning posture of activist ideology was deeply problematic for young impressionable minds such as mine. After completing what fondly refer to as my 'slit your wrists' degrees, I left university utterly nihilistic and without any answers although I had been led to believe that I knew it all, I was woke.

As it turned out, my undergrad was not only depressing it was also useless, I needed a job, so I returned to study education and began teaching in 2007. When I got to the classroom I was shocked to find I had grown up in somewhat of a bubble. I found the contract for teaching and learning had largely been torn up. I worked in low socioeconomic schools and found many children suffering from traumatic life situations. Indeed, the breaking of the contract was not unfair, these kids had far more hefty issues on their mind than learning about how to draw a neat graph or the timeline of Ancient Egypt.

I struggled on in teaching but became interested in psychology and mental health as this was the skill set I was using most of the time. Although I loved to teach, I wanted to be where I would be of most use and I thought this may be as a guidance counsellor. In 2014 I went back again to study psychology. In 2021 I graduated with first-class honours in the field of wellbeing. During this time, whilst tutoring homeschoolers, I discovered this thing called 'Classical education' and became increasingly convinced by its benefits, particularly as I discovered an explicit link between the original purpose for Classical education and human flourishing or wellbeing.

Through this journey into Classical education, the Great books and Liberal Arts tradition I gradually became aware of the major philosophical shifts in the West since the enlightenment, that resulted in an inexorable shift away from the acceptance of reality on its own terms and instead the pursuit of external Utopian ideals. I came to realise that the nihilism and psychological chaos that had infected my thinking throughout my studies were the product of a system of thought, that purports that reality can be shaped into an ideal that will lead to a just society and human flourishing. This system derives from a number of sources; socialism, cultural Marxism, deconstructionism, that can be generally classified as critical theory. I will briefly discuss how this is incommensurate with psychological wellbeing and argue how the renewal of Classical education is an expression of what I call true human culture and maybe the only cultural response equipped to draw us back toward wisdom, harmony, and human flourishing.

HOW AND WHY WESTERN CULTURE HAS COME TO EMBRACE NOTIONS OF ARTIFICIAL REALITY: THE EMPEROR – AN UNWISE RULER

To begin a quick psychological profile of some characters in one of our favourite parable, the emperor's new clothes. We know how it goes; we learn of a emperor who is taken in by swindlers. They successfully play him to invert his perception of reality, to believe in something that was not real to the extent that he loses much of his wealth and all his dignity. So, in the emperor we see the image of a vain incompetent character. One not interested in leadership or responsibility. He is only interested in fashion.

From a psychological perspective, he is a mess, he lacks meaning, purpose and moral direction. He is materialistic, hedonistic, and self-obsessed (sound familiar?). His poor sense of self leads him to constantly seek external affirmation and he can't seem to face up to the reality of his job as king, he is striving for validation on Instagram, he has superficial friendships and is surrounded by 'yes' men. If, in the emperor we see an image of modern Western civilisation, we can guess that he also lacks a loving, personalised relationship with a creator God, and derives a sense of self only from the immediate material universe. It has been argued that the unpairing of the Western worldview from Christian Theism through the enlightenment, produced a society of self-interested actors, superficial and disconnected from their spiritual and cultural heritage, lacking in shared values or social cohesion (Dawson, _). Psychologically, the emperor is suffering symptoms associated with psychological distress and as such he is vulnerable and at risk of exploitation and manipulation by bad actors. Which is where the story goes next.

THE SWINDLERS – A DENUNCIATION
OF REALITY

The story continues as the swindlers arrive in town, selling just the product that the emperor so desires, he's been scrolling, he's seen the ads, he feels the hype and knows that this thing they are offering will satisfy that hollow feeling in his chest, it will fulfil and make him whole and finally give his life meaning. Its marketing 101, identify a deficit, problematise reality by amplifying negative truths like 'racism' or 'sexism' and exploit society's state of immaturity and superficiality, by presenting a product that is actually not fit for purpose, because the goal is not justice but takeover.

So we quickly find some big problems with the proposed solution, The Swindlers: 'boast of a wonderful cloth, with the virtue of being invisible to anyone who was stupid or not fit to hold their position'. But the product doesn't exist. The Voice proponents have executed this strategy in amplifying Aboriginal injustice and presenting a Utopian solution, short on detail, but not actually fit for purpose.

James Lindsay says it like this, 'Negation of the real is established by creating an interpretive frame that deliberately cause people to misunderstand reality – disconnecting one from reality through its images and constructs.' The real is then replaced with a 'hyperreal simulation', the invisible cloth (gender fluidity, antiracism, equity, diversity and inclusion), a Utopian promise that never actualises.

Interestingly, Lindsay teases out a genesis of 'negative thinking' from the enlightenment, as faith was gradually replaced with cartesian methodology and the rise of science. This sceptical approach originates in scientific method debunking untruths using the null hypothesis. This project morphed into a generalised critical approach to knowledge and fused with socialist principals around power into critical theory and deconstructionism which has arguably come to dominate all fields of academic endeavour.

In wokeism the negative thinking paradigm has reached a hysterical climax. 'Woke denunciation' replaces the scientific negative critique. Paulo Freire, an educational theorist, the father of woke, called for a perpetual revolution of pure criticism and permanent denunciation of the world. This state of perpetual revolution is an extremely disorienting experience and I speak from personal experience here. Without being able to get a fix on what is real, the young, indoctrinated student is left with only a sense of grievance where the only acceptable response is through activism.

Without a solid grounding in cultural heritage, without a sense of identity or story (because education in history and humanities has been politicised, deconstructed and fragmented), young students in the West, are very vulnerable to this indoctrination they, like the emperor lack the moral or intellectual maturity needed to effectively detect and respond to the negative critique and emotional denunciations of their world. These students, then go out to gain positions of influence in the institutions and corporations that have significant reach into culture.

Well, you know the rest of the story, the public all follow suit for a range of reasons, a cultural revolution in swing. With reality successfully denounced, 'no clothes' being successfully inverted to 'the finest suit ever', the swindlers complete their job, and promptly leave town with the booty.

THE WISDOM OF THE CHILD – HOPE RETURNS

When we look at the end of the story, when the emperor has totally given up his dignity and manhood to the woke crowd, we see a call back to reality in the form of a child. Now, as any parent knows, children have incredible skill at seeing and saying reality as it is, and this ability, says Josef Pieper is the definition of wisdom. The child, not yet indoctrinated to doubt his lying eyes, is the one who is wise. However, the wisdom of the child is where Hans Christian Anderson leaves us in this tale.

Two points summarise the significance of this parable; the emperor as image of an average citizen is ill-equipped, and vulnerable to manipulation and exploitation because of his materialistic worldview and poor moral formation, and a manufactured reality, a hyperreality, has become normalised, preferable and actively promoted by its proponents for the purpose of power. So, the next question we face is how to equip our young people against this twisted version of reality?

WELLBEING – THE NEW HOLY GRAIL

Let's turn for a moment to examine, the concept of psychological wellbeing. This term is interchangeable with two other terms in the contemporary psychological literature, flourishing and eudaimonia. Eudaimonia was defined by Aristotle as the ultimate goal and highest good for human beings. It is not the result of external circumstance or 'feel goods' (though these have their place). To achieve eudaimonia one must fulfill their purpose and develop their rational and moral capacities to the fullest potential. Augustine and Aquinas reframed Aristotelian eudaimonia within the Christian worldview, and the means by which the development of these capacities was achieved? Education. For Aristotle, Augustine, and Aquinas eudaimonia or human flourishing was sole purpose of education.

Skip forward to the 20th /21st century and we see an explosion in the wellbeing movement promoted by researchers such as Martin Seligman. In the last 30 years wellbeing has come to dominate psychological discourse in response to the increasing epidemic of mental illness (20% of Australians being diagnosed with mental illness in their life). Seligman's wellbeing model proposes 5 'evidence-based' domains associated with eudaimonia; positive emotion, engagement (or flow), positive relationships, meaning/ purpose and accomplishment (mastery). So, a eudemonic or flourishing individual is ticking boxes in all of these domains. If we think back to the emperor aka western society deficits across many if not all of these are obvious. Student wellbeing was cited as one of the major issues of concerns in the recent review by the Productivity Commission (Jan 2023) on education and obviously, is directly related to other metrics such as literacy and numeracy standard, school attendance etc. clearly, the critical theory approach to reality is doing a poor job of producing eudemonic citizens.

The link between ancient philosophy and modern conceptualisations of wellbeing highlights the key role that education should play in the formation of psychologically stable humans and is an indictment of changes that have led to recent failures. If education is the mechanism by which culture is transmitted, then it is truly ground zero in the cultural and psychological crises facing society. I would like to propose Classical education in the Liberal Arts Tradition, or as I call it, *true human culture* as the best and possibly only response to issues associated with culture, wokeism, and wellbeing.

A RESPONSE - WHAT IS CLASSICAL EDUCATION AND THE LIBERAL ARTS TRADITION?

To define Classical education I will use the following metaphor. Two sentences; 'The carpenter *planes* the wood'. 'The rose *blooms.*' If we focus on the verbs in each of these sentences we see in the first *'planes'* is a **transitive** verb; the action begins with the carpenter and ends with the wood, the action is external. In the second, the verb *'blooms'* is an **intransitive** verb; the action of blooming begins and ends with the rose for the purpose of its fullness. This lovely analogy succinctly demonstrates that where modern education is aimed towards employment and external goods, it is utilitarian, classical education's orientation is human flourishing.

Classical education (CE) WAS the mainstream mode of education for best part of two thousand years and as such is as 'evidence-based' as you can get. Tolstoy deftly diagnoses the perils associated with the move away from this traditional mode in his novel Anna Karenina. Karenin declares that 'the new scientific education would be desirable if it wasn't totally amoral and producing nihilism.' 150 years on and we sadly see CE has nevertheless been replaced by a scientific mode of education and so an exercise in archaeology is required if we are to rediscover this lost tradition.

CLASSICAL EDUCATION
AS TRUE HUMAN CULTURE

Whilst in classical education, we are talking about a cultural tradition originating in Ancient Greece and subsequently the Christian West, I have come to regard it as a quality expression of true human culture. This universal nature lies in its philosophical roots. CE is predicated on a process of revelation and discovery of that which is beautiful, true and good and is fundamentally linked to the concept of the *logos*; an idea that the universe is founded in an order that is coherent, knowable and benevolent. For the early church fathers this concept was revealed as the Christ and thereupon was formed an incredible cultural flexibility whereby human flourishing and fullness was discovered through the stories, myth and traditions of the lands where it grew. This is why examples of 'the Canon' emerge from such culturally diverse backgrounds as Homer's *Odyssey*, to the Anglo-Saxon *Beowulf* or Arthurian tales, to Native American tales like *Hiawatha* and more recently Indian myth and Chinese philosophy have been acknowledged as aligned to the CE project. C.S. Lewis's exposition of this logos was articulated in his work the *Abolition of Man*. Thus the CE project seeks to synthesise both the unity and diversity of the human experience through the search for objective truth.

Over the course of the past 40 years, the United States has seen a renewal of the CE project, giving rise to many schools, curricula and philosophical publications on the subject. The book *Liberal Arts Tradition* by Kevin Clark and Ravi Jain, provides a well-rounded and detailed basis for understanding the CE tradition as it existed from late-antiquity to the early modern era, connecting it to the contemporary classroom and community. I will briefly touch on a few principles from this work to highlight key counter-cultural departures in CE from modern education. These can be thought of as cultural starting points rather than classroom curriculum. They act to restore humanity and wholeness to the education project and fall under an umbrella term, poetic knowledge.

POETIC KNOWLEDGE –
PIETY, MUSIC, GYMNASTIC

Piety is an unpleasant term in the modern context, associated with a holier-than-thou-Reverend-Brocklehurst-in-Jane-Eyre disposition. However, for ancient and medieval people, piety was a foundational precept for society and motivating factor for the education system. In essence piety means self is second to duty, in Christian parlance it is 'fear of the Lord'. A dutiful disposition toward one's faith, family and society (in that order) which frames a moral world order. Piety was conveyed via *paideia* a wraparound term for education and enculturation and the method for cultural transmission. The Roman translation for paideia is *humanitas*, meaning what it is to be human, human culture. Piety forms the foundational frame for paideia in that it shapes proper loves, through the articulation of beliefs, values and virtues. Thus piety orders right relationship of the individual toward God, family and society, it represents an education in love and the beginning of wisdom.

Gymnastic is the principle of an embodied reality. The belief that training the body was good for the mind and soul. In the ancient world, subjugation of the body through training had important practical implications for biological survival, however the redeemed Christian view of creation offered a more loving view of physical nature, not only for the purpose of sustaining life but as a vehicle to discern, celebrate and participate in creation. With the arrival of Cartesian thought *'I think therefore I am'* in the Enlightenment, this unified body mind relationship was fractured. Consciousness was reoriented away from the sensed world elevating pure thought. CE in the Liberal Arts Tradition upholds the value of gymnastic and its role in perception of reality, as it is, through the senses. This important principle of embodied learning is deeply relevant to our current context. An embodied orientation is like an insurance policy against the swindler that require a denial of the senses, what we see, hear and feel in order to perpetrate the hyperreality. Gymnastic is inextricably linked to, and informed by engagement with beauty and poetic knowledge from early childhood and provides an essential point of reference for truth. Gymnastic therefore provides a basis for a well-ordered perception of reality, a connection to gut-instinct, a fidelity to poetic knowledge.

MUSIC – TUNING HEARTS TO THE REAL

'Musical training is a more potent instrument than any other, because rhythm and harmony find their way into the inward places of the soul, on which they mightily fasten, imparting grace.' (Plato, Republic III)

Music education in CE can be described as soulcraft. Carried out properly it tunes the heart and makes one perceptive to truth and goodness. A properly tuned soul is the foundation of CE tradition. Without a well-stocked moral imagination, without trained sentiment, without a heart, there can be no human flourishing. Music in this sense is broader than understood in contemporary culture and can be thought of as harmony. It incorporates *musica instrumentalis;* the music of instruments, the outward expression or vehicle through which to comprehend the principle. *Musica mundana,* music of the world, signifies the principle of an ordered, harmonious and orchestrated universe and *musica humana,* the principle of harmony within and between the humans. As a music teacher, I have witnessed the immediate impacts of harmony in a classroom settings.

The foundational frame of piety, gymnastic and music can be summarised as poetic knowledge. In contrast to rational or scientific knowledge. This mode of learning prefigures the rational emphasising intuitive, natural and contemplative understandings. Poetic knowledge thus privileges the roles of wonder, curiosity, imagination, and beauty in creating a positive and moral foundation for engagement in learning and adds to this later faculties of rationality, reason and science. A reorientation of our cultural metrics and academics toward valuing this mode of knowledge, a difficult task as education systems have largely disregarded poetic knowledge and are now firmly aligned with scientific modes of knowledge.

CLASSICAL EDUCATION THE CASE FOR PSYCHOLOGICAL WELLBEING AND HUMAN FLOURISHING

In addition to poetic knowledge, CE incorporates a range of principles and practices that develop further the cultural foundations established above, that cannot be discussed thoroughly here but I will touch on a few. The seven liberal arts formed an approach to curriculum that focussed on development of intellectual and moral rigour in both the language and mathematical arts. Two key points here are that they were arts to be mastered iteratively over time, they were more generalist than specialist but were especially demanding in the areas of memory, language and speech. Secondly, they were aimed at producing liberated individuals, who understood their sovereign identity as created within a divine purpose, a deep sense of humanity and the ability to express this identity within the polity. In addition to the liberal arts, several other key ideas in CE contribute not only to a well-educated citizenry, but also psychological well-being.

The chronological teaching of history acts to establish students' sense of self within the grand narrative resulting in a worldview that is understandable, cohesive, and ordered, traits that give rise to resilient and stable humans with solid identity formation based on shared beliefs which are essential for positive relationships and prosocial behaviour.

The *humanitas* approach means an integrated, narrative approach to schooling that acts to increase student engagement because it focusses less on scientific accumulation of disembodied facts and more on knowledge through the 'grand narrative'. Humans are relational beings, whose memory and deep learning are activated through interconnections and relationship. When framed as story, students are given the opportunity to engage vicariously in relationships and experiences of those who have gone before them. Such experiential learning even of the imagined kind is known to be the most powerful mode of learning possible, with increased encoding and retention of knowledge. Think learning to cook by reading a recipe vs actually cooking. Whilst a bunch of disembodied facts may be interesting, they will not be alive like they are when embedded in story, this is what Charlotte Mason called 'Living Books'. This approach derived in CE from the oral histories of ancient Greece and Europe is comparable to oral transmission used by traditional societies such as the Song lines and myth cycles in Indigenous Australian knowledge systems.

Multum non multa (much not many) and *festina lente* (make haste slowly) are related principles that act to recalibrate content selection, reducing specialisation and allowing for mastery. It means identifying and prioritising foundational knowledge deeply rather than the crammed curriculum that plagues Australian classrooms. This means students have opportunity to understand and fix mistakes and experience mastery and a sense of accomplishment which Seligman identified as a domain of wellbeing. In a crowded, frantic curriculum, mastery is a fleeting chance limited to only a few. Connected to these is the principle of *schole*. This Greek term from which *school* is derived is known as the principle of restful learning. Related to concepts of contemplation and leisure it priorities time and space for peaceful encounters with knowledge, is often connected to experiences of the natural environment and can equate to notions of mindfulness, positive emotion and spiritual connection.

Virtue and character formation are central goals for CE and is expressed in the intentional selection of content and skills that are characterised by objectively 'good' characters. These provide powerful models for social learning. One contemporary example may be the thinking skills associated with cognitive behavioural therapies (CBT) which directly draw upon the stoic tradition of Ancient Rome. Thus, selection of works by Emperor Marcus Aurelius will embed the same skills valued by every CBT therapist in Australia.

Whilst most Australians understand the difficulties faced by young people in schools and society generally the identification and remedy of these problems are difficult as the normalised worldview, the post-Enlightenment critical, scientific approach to reality is itself the problem. Thus, the proposition of Classical education is actually one of radical cultural reform; this is a good thing, it is needed. We do not want our children to be nihilistic, superficial and self-obsessed. We need them to be whole, well-ordered, filled with a sense of shared humanity and equipped with skills and knowledge to walk out their freedom and purpose in accordance with the logos.

Classical education in the liberal arts tradition is a call to community and culture not just curriculum, it is a positive construct with achievable goals. We are unsure what it looks like, that's because culture is a combination of living change and tradition, there is no quick dummies guide or shortcuts, it requires some intellectual and emotional heavy lifting to enter into new collegial friendships, to intentionally form communities of sometimes disparate characters in faith. We all are implicated in the failures of the West, perhaps we have not loved enough, perhaps we have been too comfortable in our own echo chambers, the Classical tradition is a call to mission and I am convinced that is the prime vehicle by which we can grow a hopeful future, founded in ancient universal wisdom that combines faith and reason, poetics and science in balance for correct discernment of reality as it is, at once imperfect and good.

UNHISTORICAL ACTS OF EVERYMAN: RISING FROM THE SLUMBER OF INERTIA

Karina Hepner

ABSTRACT

History has repeatedly demonstrated moments where one group has sought to dominate another group's actions, beliefs and values. From antiquity to the Middle Ages to the twentieth century, some sources have identified these periods as a dark, deadly hour. Today is no different. In this modern climate where individuals fear questioning accepted notions or avoid challenging dominant narratives, how then should they proceed? Much like courageous groups and individuals from the past, often the obscure Everyman, the way forward is to become the hope and be the difference.

For they all were trying to make us afraid, saying, 'Their hands will be weakened in the work, and it will not be done.' Now therefore, O God, strengthen my hands. (Nehemiah 6:9)

In December last year, the World Economic Forum, the self-appointed guardian of the universe, collected from online dictionaries the five most searched for words in 2022:

1.   War.
2.   Permacrisis.
3.   Woman.
4.   Gaslighting.
5.   Goblin Mode.

Young, British writer Esmé Partridge in her article, 'The Death of Ideals', offers this definition of goblin mode, the least known of these terms:

> '... *the antithesis of being that girl who embodies productivity, wellness and aesthetic perfection, an unleashing of the creature within [and] shamelessly embracing your inner slob.'* [44]

In essence, this mode rejects the idealised, self-doctored persona platformed on Insta. While not all of us would feel liberated to sit on the floor in yesterday's pjs, eating rice like popcorn, this passive resistance reflects the purposeless drift of today. To be a slob is to have blurred vision, an *ennui* to the global values that generate human flourishing. Contrarily, actively resisting the Ministry of Progressive Culture has a stinging price. Renegades who openly question the dominant narratives risk being silenced, cancelled and de-platformed. They may even be showered with tomato soup.

But perhaps the Empire of Hurt Feelings or Victimhood (Non) Anonymous is a stimulant for Everyman to do something urgently? Perhaps this *nouveau* cultural imperialism smashing through institutions, toppling statues, de-colonising and 'greening' school curricula, curating online activity, re-programming the mind of the public and creating puppet politicians and CEOs is precisely part of a Divine Plan in order for us to seek after and find all that is true, honest, just, pure, lovely and virtuous? Indeed, it is too easy to tell of the stuff and nonsense that haunts our lives and disrupts our sleep. The winds of corruption and confusion blow at will.

44   Patridge, E. 'The Death of Ideals: TikTok, goblin mode, and the end of Platonism.' *The Critic*, 4 August 2022. https://thecritic. co.uk/the-death-of-ideals/

Once hidden desires, whispered in secret, are now paraded, delighted in during daylight. Paradoxically, we also require trigger warnings, microaggression awareness and 'white fragility' de-programming. This muddled thinking is like a virus, deadly and highly contagious, a super-spreader, and it's indiscriminate as to whom it infects. Its symptoms are the muzzling of robust, rigorous conversations on things that matter most. We wring our hands. What is one to do with this double, double toil and trouble?

Interestingly, history repeatedly demonstrates what needs to be done when all things appear midnight dreary. Throughout the ages, where toil and trouble seem to reign supreme, goodness becomes the weapon of choice, disrupting vain attempts to subvert the Divine Order of a Grand Design. And you and I have a significant role to play in our spheres of influence; each of us has been placed at this exact moment in time for a purpose.

Let's firstly revisit the Roman Empire in the first two and a half centuries: indomitable, militarily invincible, affluent and dictatorial. As a polytheistic society, the Roman leadership frowned upon its subjects failing to sacrifice to their state gods. In fact, such failure was treason. Yet there were the infidels, mostly unnamed, the converts of the early church, refusing to worship the gods of the day. Without their courage, Divine Truth would have forked no lightning. Our primary evidence of their stories is sparse, of course, however, Justin the Philosopher or Justin Martyr, who converted to Christianity in about 130AD, writes of his new cultural group, Christians, submitting to death rather deny their convictions: 'though beheaded and crucified and thrown to wild beasts and chains and fire and all other kinds of torture, we do not give up our confession'.[45] To waver from the accepted practices of the

45   St. Justin Martyr, chapter 109 in *Dialogue with Trypho, Early*

Roman Empire was often deadly. In 250AD, Dionysius of Alexandria writes to the Bishop of Antioch where he speaks of these believers in a new religion, the matrons and maidens, soldiers and civilians,

> ... *the multitudes of those who had to wander about in desert places and upon the mountains, and who were cut off by hunger, and thirst, and cold, and sickness, and robbers, and wild beasts.*[46]

These largely nameless people walked with boldness, through much suffering, but with much conviction. The early believers were the representation of Roman resentments and anxieties because they refused to honour the gods that allegedly had gifted *Imperium Romanum* with affluence and prosperity. Today, refusing to pay homage to the unholy trinity of gender, race and climate change invites gnashing of cyber-teeth. A fourth-century, well-educated bishop, Athanasius of Alexandria, lived in the hub of intellectualism, but spoke out against the increasing unsettled Roman rule. He encountered much persecution, false accusations and repeated exiles for his beliefs, and yet he would not be silenced. Despite brutal forces against him, he was able to write, 'For, indeed, everything about is marvellous, and wherever a man turns his gaze he sees the Godhead of the Word and is smitten with awe.'[47]

Overall, these early historical tales tell us of men and women, from all walks of life, remaining steadfast, not

Christian Writings, http://www.earlychristianwritings.com/text/justinmartyr-dialoguetrypho.html

46   Dionysius of Alexandria, 'Epistle iii. --To Fabius, Bishop of Antioch', https://www.newadvent.org/cathen/05011a.htm

47   St Athanasius. 'Refutation of the Gentiles Chapter 8'. *On the Incarnation of the Word.* https://www.ccel.org/ccel/athanasius/incarnation.ix.html

vanquishing their responsibility to re-shape culture. Professor Henry van Til, a Calvinist College professor provoked his readership into action in his 1959 *magnus opus: Does the twentieth-century disciple have a right to discard the cultural mandate, twice given to the human race, by Jehovah Himself? Are we justified in turning the world and culture over to the enemies of God? How far does the kingship of Christ extend?*[48]

From antiquity to the Middle Ages, history offers other stories of goodness emerging from oppression. Perhaps this character's mythography has swallowed some of the truth of the tale, yet Jeanne d'Arc or Joan of Arc, a daughter of an obscure tenant farmer in the village of Domrémy, modern Lorraine, becomes a trope for boldness and hope, despite unconquerable odds. According to a Parisian eyewitness from the 1400s, the sufferings of his fellow citizens during the 100 years' War was intensely violent. Only known as Bourgeois of Paris, his now published diary from 1405-1449 recounts that the Armagnacs were ruthlessly killed by axes or other weapons in the streets where the dead were left in piles, and homes were full of the victims, brutally slain.[49] Such was the chaos that wolves would roam the streets, feasting upon the rotting corpses. These were terrifying days for France under English rule. In 1492, divinely inspired by visions of the saints, country-girl Jeanne d'Arc led the French army in a momentous victory at Orléans, repulsing an English attempt to conquer France during this Hundred Years' War. She brought hope to a demoralised army. She valued obedience to that which was good and noble over personal comfort. She

48   Van Til, H. *The Calvinistic Concept of Culture.* Baker Bookhouse, 1959. p.22

49   Shirley, Janet (translator). *A Parisian Journal, 1405-1449.* Clarendon P, 1968.

stood up for truth. Yet much worked against her: her age, her gender, her education, her social status. However, she rose above the social and political mores of her dark days. The transcripts of her interrogation make for disturbing reading: each time her worldly-wise interrogators, Cauchon, bishop of Beauvais, and Jean Lemaître, the vice-inquisitor of France crafted questions to confuse her, the 19-year-old peasant girl answered with calm precision. Geoffrey Thérage, Jeanne's executioner, later confessed that she had been tied too high to the scaffold to drive a stake through her heart, as was the custom before burning heretics. When the flames licked at her feet, she screamed, 'Jesus', until her body fell limp. Surely, he had put to death a martyr, Thérage later mused. Douglas Murray, UK political commentator and journalist in his 2019 book, *The Madness of Crowds*, tells his readers that society is paralysed by fear, and we have 'unlearned' the ability to speak candidly about the things that matter most. Surely, Jeanne of Arc's story can re-teach us how then we should live.

For the final historical example of boldness, we enter a time of groupthink, mass formation, media control and anti-intellectualism. This was 1940s Poland, under Nazi control. Meet Auschwitz-Burkinau prisoner 41335, Stanislawa Leszczyńska captured by the Gestapo for forging papers for the Jews desperate to escape a nearby Polish ghetto. Stanislawa was a trained mid-wife, whose qualifications were discovered in the camp, forcing her to be used in the makeshift 'maternity' ward for two years until liberation in 1945. Prior to her arrival, 100s of prisoners' babies were cruelly aborted or immediately murdered by drowning them in a barrel of icy water and thrown away Although difficult to total, roughly 3000 babies were born alive, delivered into Stanislawa's caring hands. While the infants' fate thereafter was often adoption or death, the mothers were provided with some joy and comfort of holding their precious offspring. Stanislawa was affectionately known as 'mother' or 'angel'. After liberation, Stanislawa's folded quietly back into Polish life, continuing her midwifery and caring for her family, rarely speaking of her prison days. In the late 1950s, however, she delivered a paper on 2 March during a Polish midwives' jubilee held in the health department of the Bałuty district of the city of Łódź. In this report, she detailed her death camp years, acknowledging the selfless acts of imprisoned, medical doctors. 'What I observed,' she said, 'surpasses my ability to say what I really feel about the tremendous dignity of the physician's vocation and the heroism with which they carried out their duties'.[50] She described the appalling filth of the maternity ward, the teeming vermin, rats larger than fat cats, the diseases and the biting cold. The conditions for the birthing mothers were horrific and inhumane. Miraculously, however, in her time, not one baby died at birth, and when she reported this to a Nazi officer in the camp, '[h]e looked at [her] in disbelief and said that even the best German university hospitals could not boast of such a success rate'.[51] All babies were born to term, looking healthy and normal, she explained in her 1957 report. Stanislawa died in 1974, and her funeral was a manifestation of affection and honour. Years later, in a letter, a fellow liberated prisoner reflected on her camp years with the midwife: '[Stanislawa] had the courage to defy the order of the Nazi criminals to help those of her fellow prisoners survive whose lives were in jeopardy and who had also lost their greatest treasure − their child'.[52]

50   Leszczyńska, S. A midwife's report from Auschwitz. Bałuk-Ulewiczowa, T., trans. Medical Review − Auschwitz. August 21, 2018. https://www.mp.pl/auschwitz.

51   Ibid.

52   Kłodziński, S. Stanisława Leszczyńska. Chłopicki, W., trans. *Medical Review − Auschwitz*. March 19, 2019.

While under severe restraint and oppression, she remained completely devoted to her fellow human beings. Often, she would sing hymns to uplift the spirits of the disheartened, despairing mothers. Each baby was baptised by her. She was considerate and temperate and kind. But when faced with ungodly commands to kill the babies and to dispose of their bodies like refuse, she boldly and without hesitation, told Dr Josef Mengele, the personification of wickedness, she, personally, would not follow these evil orders of the regime. Her concluding words in her midwifery report is as follows: 'I am presenting my account on behalf of the mothers and children—those who could not tell the world about the wrong done them.'[53]

So now in 2023 we find ourselves locked in the Circus Maximus of modern madness. Whilst there's no lion pacing outside our gate, no flames hungry for our bodies, no crematorium to incinerate our lives, we know there's more than one way to kill a man. You can remove his values that give him divine purpose. You can dismantle his world and create nothing better for him. You can surrender all meaning to his life, teaching and training his young mind that divine purpose is merely a fabrication: life is a continuous struggle against exploitation and subversion. You can muddle his mind, telling him evil is good and good is evil. Then you can push him into the digital town square and watch the keyboard pitch forks remove his heart, pluck out his eyes and pull out his tongue. Of course, for him, the consequence of this re-programming is goblin mode or coercion to join an angry mob. But the historical men and women referenced in this paper have also lived with immense difficulties; yet they illuminated a brighter way. Surely, we too must become lightning to our own troubling days. We can no longer fret

53   Ibid.

over potential personal suffering in defending goodness nor yawn at the slithering threats to our freedoms lest we encounter hardships or hate. If we stand for nothing, we'll fall for everything and bring a crowd with us.

On a practical level, we are buoyed by emerging communities of goodness that offer reason, truth and genuine learning. It begins in the classroom. All over the country, we have inspirational educators busily building better. They are devoted to reclaiming education, establishing new schools with a bright future. Several schools await expectantly to open their doors to children. Their learning framework features logic and intellectual richness, fighting back against the ideologically-driven practices and illogical compliance commands that have infected globalised education. These Australian neo-classical or liberal art schools, emerging in many states, will provide opportunities for pupils to think, to reason, to question. Through the breeze of good books, often old books, the pupils will find stories of the human condition: love, redemption, aspiration, conflict, death, resurrection, joy, suffering, vicissitude, endurance, compassion, and hope. These new schools need our support.

Another practical step to create positive community change is to join the nation-wide organisation, Street Level Australia, founded by Milly Maine. It aims to prevent the barbaric slough of urban ugliness. This group with 'chapters' in several Australian cities supports and encourages projects that feature beautiful architecture and advocates for classical planning and human-centred spaces to promote human flourishing. By being connected to these like-minded thinkers, members will learn how to communicate well with local developers and town councils to suggest ways to transform concrete boxes into inspiring symbols of classical beauty in their towns and cities.

And finally, on a local level, why not offer your living room or kitchen table as a welcoming space with your neighbours to wrestle with taboo topics? A recent online conversation about positive cultural change had this father share his contribution: 'I have been doing a weekly gathering called 'Dinner at Dad's house' for my [high-school] age son and his friends and my college-age daughter and her friends. I make a great meal, then as we eat, I ask questions to get them to think. I have upwards of 15 young people each week. My goal is simply to get them to question what the culture is saying to them...'.[54] Seventeenth-century poet, John Donne, opined that 'No man is an island entire of itself; every man / is a piece of the continent, a part of the main'. People desperately seek connection; they want to be heard and to be seen. They desire genuine face-to-face time with others to counteract a world where individual identity is swallowed by the Machine of data-collection and invasive surveillance.

In all, we cannot wait for a Joan of Arc nor a Polish midwife nor our politicians to lead the way. There is no cavalry waiting to defend you. The historical characters referenced in this paper were the heroes for *their day*, yet utterly oblivious to their legacy. Much of the thought in this paper is predicated on the final line of George Elliot's novel, *Middlemarch*, 'for the growing good of the world is partly dependent on unhistoric acts; and that things are not so ill with you and me as they might have been is half owing to the number who lived faithfully a hidden life, and rest in unvisited tombs'.[55] For this hour, you're the hero. You have been placed here for a purpose at this time in this location at

54   Johnson, B. *Keys to Influence, Walking in both Divine Wisdom and Supernatural Power*. Bill Johnson Teaching, online discussion. 5 October, 2023.

55   Eliot, G. *Middlemarch*. Penguin Books, 1994, p. 838.

precisely the right moment. Indeed, we may never hold a live debate with Yuval Noah Harari, Israeli intellectual, the bald, golden-haired boy of the WEF or fight as a general in the Russian vs Ukrainian war. Maybe some will. Perhaps it's not so much about winning the public debate or military war as it is living the difference by maintaining what you know is right in the face of corrupted values.

Today, we need to become a hopeful signifier wherever we have been placed – in our homes, in our workspaces, in our friends' lives. Rise from inertia. Demonstrate truth. Create and build. Magnify goodness. Fear not but love much. Become the inoculation to the trouble at hand. Those early believers, a poor French girl and an obscure, Polish midwife were not raptured away to safety when things became too hard, nor did they hold official positions of title and power. Tolstoy realised that the kingdom of God was within us and within reach of us all. Heaven, so understands Goethe's Faust, was not just a place but the end of striving; it was inspired divine action. Become love in action. By being the antithesis of the cultural chaos of our time, we emerge as hope personified.

QUIET BUSINESSES NEED TO SPEAK UP

Daniel Lewkovitz

ABSTRACT

Traditionally there were three things one never discussed in the workplace: Sex, Religion and Politics. Over the last decade two of those formally taboo subjects - sex and politics, have not only found their way into the workplace, they've become mandatory and highly visible requirements for virtue signalling corporations. Even though this may fly in the face of the third taboo - religion, and workers who previously did not have to contemplate the sexuality of the person sitting next to them at work. It is now inadequate to merely abhor racism or be tolerant of others. The new right-on obligations of businesses are to make what should be unnecessary public statements. That they abhor racism, or that they are committed to saving the planet from apocalyptic global warming all while waving rainbow flags. Never mind the inconvenient fact that - usually when nobody is looking - they outsource their manufacturing to human-rights abusing countries for whom racism, pollution or executing homosexuals is standard practice. Business is business, right?

Increasingly large corporations are subject to ESG (environmental and social governance) scores which affect their ability to trade, borrow and invest. ESG, also known as 'corporate woke', 'social justice' or a new form of 'governance' have become highly valuable tools for companies to cover their other failures and incompetence.

This needs to stop. However business owners have been cowed into silence. With few exceptions, business owners won't say in public what they believe in private. They remain silent for fear of being cancelled by a frothing mob and the resultant harm they believe it can cause their companies. But is the threat real?

This presentation will study what really happens when good businesses speak out, and why they must. If you don't rock the boat you will go down with it.

The nexus between the Community, Business and Corporate Activism has evolved in an unhealthy manner. Where traditionally, it would be enough for business to have a relationship with its community through philanthropy or sponsorships – this type of community service is now being made out to be inadequate by advocates of the recent DEI/ ESG regime. Businesses today are no longer expected to merely 'do good' – as so many do in any successful country - but are now being coercively compelled to also be 'seen to be doing good'.

This is not just the plight of multinational corporations as might be anticipated, and the shockwaves have permeated all the way through to small Mum and Dad businesses in Australia. All elements of Australian businesses, be they small or large are now experiencing considerable pressure to *loudly* display their goodness through a constant flurry of virtue signalling or face potentially disastrous consequences. Its pervasive nature means a belief that the failure of an Australian business to participate in it will result in customers failing to engage with this business' products or an inability of this business to be able to attract and retain staff.

Any fair-minded person would have to ask – *why* is this happening?

Why are companies going out of their way to be *seen* to be doing good?

If you visit nearly any small café, local mechanic or butcher shop, a wall will be covered in thank you certificates and letters from local primary schools and sporting clubs who've benefited from the business's support or sponsorship. Perhaps someone donated a meat tray or fixed the dodgy school bus or sponsored the athletics team. Companies doing good work in their local community is nothing new.

Small businesses like these, or companies like mine, quietly get on with doing good work, helping customers and the community and perhaps being profitable. Small businesses have always done it tough in this country, despite which they're usually trying to do the right thing. But that's no longer enough. Now you have to actually be an activist. It's not enough to merely dislike mistreatment of people, oppose sexism, abhor racism or violence against women. I don't think there's many business leaders in 2024 who liked any of those things to begin with.

Larger companies now feel an obligation to loudly proclaim their dislike for such things in every aspect of their operations. The scale at which larger companies now purport to do this is off the charts and likely out of all proportion to how much they are benefiting the community or society. Particularly, in the case of banks and investment funds, when compared to the potential dollar value this might represent.

A new feature on the corporate landscape is 'Environmental, Social and corporate Governance' (ESG). This is why every company you've ever heard of now has a 35-page plan to improve social awareness and improve 'sustainability' in order to literally change the climate and save the planet.

Apparently all a consumer need do is support the respective business and soon the world will be free of racism, sexism and especially climate change. Despite the hot air these claims typically represent. This project has commodified simple decency and propagated a thriving economy of virtue.

While plenty of companies – particularly in first-world, capitalist economies – have generally tried to minimise their environmental impact, now to address climate change and ESG obligations they must take additional steps which often include mandatory reporting to new government departments and quangos on the steps they have taken.

The best definition I've heard for the term 'woke' is: authoritarian political correctness. ESG has been described as 'corporate woke' and as an equation - the higher your ESG score is, the more 'woke' you are. There's big money in this and the money is the scariest part because it's no longer about companies quietly looking to do good or to do the right thing as it once was. It's about companies being *seen* to do good - this is because the more that you are *seen* to do the right thing the higher your ESG score goes.

So fashion labels in Australia will virtue signal to the local market by having gender non-binary, mixed race models in all of their advertising and labels on their garments saying 'This label is made from recycled plastic bottles'. The staff at the local office of the fashion brand will post to social media about an International Women's Day cupcake luncheon they attended, promote anti-racism initiatives and once or twice a year briefly cover everything in rainbows to support LGBTQI+ initiatives.

What they won't tell you is that the clothes themselves were made in a Chinese forced labour camp, often by children. So Black Lives Matter, but Uighur lives don't. Australian women deserve better but Chinese women, living in factories, getting paid far less than men and exposed to deadly chemicals – well, they don't.

It's also why if you ordered something from Amazon.com during Pride Month, it would turn up in a cardboard box that had a big rainbow around it. Inside that box would be something that was probably made by a Uighur slave in China. Amazon and Kmart would talk all about their environmental policies while selling tonnes of plastic, shipped here on a diesel belching cargo ship and shortly destined for landfill. Retailers bathe themselves in a green halo while simultaneously selling crap that nobody needs (at prices they can't resist).

For every Australian who smugly sits in their electric car, convinced they're saving the planet and making the world a better place for their children, there is someone else's children – six- year-olds in Central Africa – digging in a mine to extract cobalt for that car's batteries.

Companies are increasingly feeling the pressure to *appear* socially responsible. The concept of 'authenticity' is important in marketing, but it can be difficult for companies to reconcile these perceived social expectations, with their bottom line. This is the root of the hollowness of ESG, where companies try to appear more ethical than they perhaps are.

THE UNINTENDED CONSEQUENCES OF ESG

This approach has also had the unintended consequence of impacting the minority members of the community which it is purportedly seeking to assist. Here's a thought exercise which we've seen before - imagine a highly capable, highly competent woman who's worked her backside off to get ahead. She is now in a senior management role and there will always be people who wonder if she got there because of some affirmative action quota. This is the paradox of the ESG/ DEI movement –in its haste for affirmative action, it has instead produced a wildly unfair and disrespectful outcome.

All this imposed diversity and supposed equality eventually comes back to hurt people who've worked really hard and that's not right. And people aren't saying so because they're afraid that it's going to be a career killer.

We are now in a world where people who'd once be considered stuffy white conservatives are potentially the new counterculture against a large throng of young trendies, who are all marching in intellectual lock-step and taught *what* to think, but not *how* to think.

Whether it's on campus or in the boardroom, when only one voice and one view get heard, the other voices and the other view get smaller and smaller, and it becomes scarier and scarier to speak out. Sadly, there are some – particularly from the so-called 'progressive' side who are excited about this. I am not. They feel that unacceptable views (formerly known as an argument) are to be silenced and deplatformed.

There is now a total disconnect between what people hear, what people believe, and what people are allowed to say. By entrenching silence and subverting argumentation this has produced the greatest rate of disengagement and chronic disillusionment we have perhaps ever witnessed as a species.

It was not always this way.

WHAT DO A JEWISH BUSINESS OWNER, AN ARCHBISHOP AND A LESBIAN GOTH HAVE IN COMMON?

Once upon a time there were three things that were simply not discussed in the workplace. Ever. These were sex, religion and politics. I have experienced people's ability to stick to this rule, first hand. I founded a security business named Calamity (calamity.com.au). In 2008 my company was engaged by the Catholic Church to provide the security for World Youth Day, including the visit to Australia by The Pope.

I am fairly certain I'd be one of very few Jewish business owners in Australia carrying a letter of appreciation from the Pope.

Finally Daniel finds a car with adequate headroom.
The Pope Mobile. Sydney, 2008.

This was the largest single event ever held in the country and was bigger than the Sydney 2000 Olympics. It required years of planning by professionals in the events industry. For those unfamiliar with the events industry, its composition is typically made up of the arts crowd – read: people who plan colourful events professionally are typically quite colourful themselves. They are (or were) rock musicians, dancers, DJs and are people who took a lot of recreational drugs in their youth - or sometimes never stopped.

Picture the boardroom table in our planning session for a Church event. There were several people in suits and ties. There was a woman in a leather biker jacket, who rolled her own ciggies and had she been asked her religious beliefs would casually mention witchcraft. Sitting right next to her was a self-styled gothic lesbian with some rather extreme facial piercings (or at least they were in 2008 but now probably something you'd see at the Apple Store). To her left the Archbishop and two nuns, wearing their habit. Then there was me and the two Jewish professionals who were running the whole event on the Catholics' behalf.

Despite our differences (some quite visible) we all had the same objective – to get the job done and ensure the event was a success. By unspoken agreement everybody focused on that mission alone. The nuns at no point would try to save anyone, and the goth lesbians and witches would at no point would try to corrupt the nuns. We probably all had thoughts on each other and I'm sure there was silent prayer or comments at after-work reflective sessions but we kept those things to ourselves and simply got the job done, well and truly. Despite huge challenges WYD08 was an extraordinary success.

I'd like to make this point clearly and early on – this happened because everybody in the room left their religion, sexuality and politics at the door.

Over the last decade there has been a marked shift in corporate politics. Now, it is no longer adequate for companies to merely do the right thing by their staff, their shareholders or their customers. That's not enough. Now companies have to show the world exactly what they're doing. Particularly, it seems in matters relating to sex and politics. They have gone from 'Don't ask, don't tell' to asking staff specifically in order that they can tell the world.

ESG AND THE COMMODITISATION
OF SEXUALITY

The surge in LGBTQI+ activism has created a further change in how businesses act towards staff. Once upon a time an employer would never in a million years dream of asking an employee or a candidate 'Are you gay?' You'd be sued. To do so would be unheard of and quite rightly so. It's nobody's damned business.

However today it's quite common for employers to ask staff their sexuality for no other reason than the ability to then boast that a particular percentage of their workforce is from an LGBTQI+ background. And in turn, commoditise this sexuality. As a result, Oreos now celebrate Pride. They're a cookie. And just one example of this.

While companies that are now discussing sex and politics in the workplace still tend to avoid discussion of religion, they are insulting those for whom religion matters. It's well and good for a company to boast its support for transgenderism or homosexuality with a view to 'making everybody feel welcome' however this may not be welcoming to staff members for whom religious belief differs.

Some might argue those God-botherers need to come into 2024 but once upon a time they could happily sit shoulder to shoulder with co-workers and their religion didn't matter, nor did the sexuality of anyone in the office sitting next to them. Nobody needed to know. But DEI has taken on an almost religious zeal which overshadows those other religions which may only have a billion or so adherents. Pity in particular the poor gay or transgender worker who simply wants to be left the hell alone to do their job instead of be 'celebrated' in this way.

Anyone who dares criticise this new religion potentially risks excommunication, that is, being 'cancelled'.

Ancient Judaeo-Christian ethical principles such as equality – for everyone - are at risk of being sidelined for a new belief that echoes Orwell's Animal Farm - that 'all animals are equal, but some are more equal than others'. Employers, in the name of 'equity' (not equality) may end up promoting people ahead of others based not on skill but on racial or sexual characteristics. This is already playing out on US university campuses. A forthcoming US Supreme Court hearing will determine whether race-conscious admissions programs at Harvard and the University of North Carolina are lawful.

In 2010, the company founded embarked on building the country's best 24/7 security monitoring operation. I wanted to hire the best and brightest staff however at that time the talent pool within the security industry was rather… shallow. I had originally built the facility to be fully wheelchair accessible on the basis that the job involved sitting in a chair for 12 hours and thus people with a disability could easily perform it. Through my introduction to disability employment services I learned that there was a massive untapped talent pool of capable individuals who simply weren't given a go by many employers. This is not a criticism of those companies by the way. Firing underperforming staff is already extremely difficult due to Australia's industrial relations system so it's understandable why companies wouldn't go chasing what they might perceive as additional headaches.

Having discovered this hidden talent pool, practically overnight Calamity was a major employee of people with disabilities. We hired quadriplegics. We hired someone who was blind. We hired a gay man with HIV. We hired burns victims and I hired them for one very simple reason: they were very good at the job I needed them to do.

CALAMITY MONITORING CENTRE

To be clear, it was not a humanitarian gesture. Sure it was a nice thing to do, but that's not why we did it. We did it for eminently commercial reasons. Despite which, a year later we won a national diversity award for employment.

Being the Founder of an award-winning diversity employer, I feel entitled to say that most corporate diversity projects are rubbish. Having won the award I was invited to a conference where I was speaking on a panel alongside another panellist who worked for major telco. He was introduced as the company's 'Diversity Champion' (there's a job title I'd hitherto never heard) and his speech was a very animated rant about that organisation's boardroom and C-suite. Apparently

C-level executives were not interested in him or diversity and he felt 'Diversity wasn't getting a seat at the table'.

He asked the audience of like-minded HR types how diversity could get a seat at that table because they didn't want to listen to him or people like him. I grabbed the microphone and said it's very simple. He and others in his field (there was a roomful of them) had never, ever articulated a business case for diversity. If you can go to the leaders of any organisation and you can clearly articulate a business case they will listen. If you can't, they won't.

Disability employment is something that I'm very passionate about. If you went to any business leader and said 'What if there was a whole talent pool that no one knows about? And what if you could hire people who are highly skilled and capable, and if you give them a job, they'll seldom leave? Is that something that would be of interest to you?' There wouldn't be a single business person that would say no.

This came as a stunning revelation to the audience who all wanted to know more. I suddenly became a darling of the disability speakers' circuit because they'd spent all these years going to business groups saying 'you really have to hire these people and give them a fair go' – and wondering why nobody ever did.

Why? Because few Australian businesses themselves gets a fair go when it comes legislation around hiring and firing. So they seldom go looking for anything they believe may make their lives harder. But put forward an evidence-based and quantifiable business case, and all of a sudden they do start listening. I have proven it.

That conference was in 2013. I recently looked my fellow speaker up. He has now spoken at the United Nations. In a little under a decade, he's gone from not getting any attention in a Sydney boardroom to getting global attention at the

United Nations saying the same thing. What a difference a decade makes.

A cynic might question whether corporations are engaging in this conduct for entirely altruistic reasons and they'd be right to do so. One of the other entrants in the diversity awards was a major investment bank who had hired a young man with Down Syndrome to work in their mailroom. Good on them for doing so. As part of their awards program submission, they produced a film showing the young man walking around the office, delivering mail and hugging and high-fiving office workers, sometimes in slow motion to a swelling orchestral score. The video would have easily cost thousands to produce and was sneered at by one of the more cynical attendees in a wheelchair as 'disability porn'.

This bank, with thousands of employees had hired one person with a disability and run straight off to their marketing and PR department. Wouldn't an award look nice? Compare that to the behaviour of my company. We were a small business, not yet profitable, that had over half its workforce with a disability. Unlike the bank we hadn't even mentioned it to anyone. This was my first exposure to corporate virtue signalling being louder than any actual good deeds to which it refers.

THE VIRTUOUS BANK

A recent experience, has shown me the dollar value of such virtue signalling.

The slogan of my company is 'Be Fearless' and 'Fearless' appears on much of our material. A year ago I received a phone call from my lawyer saying, there had been an application to IP Australia to have our trademarks removed for non-use.

It was absurd. We had used the slogan literally every single day. It was on our business cards. It was on our website. It was on our vehicles and on every email we ever sent. It represented the fearless way we conduct ourselves. Who would make such an argument? He told me the opponent was State Street Bank.

What is it with banks?

State Street is an American bank with over US$40 trillion in assets in 2023.

Some years back State Street Bank had sponsored a popular artwork that 'went viral', at the height of the #MeToo movement around the issues of sexual harassment and sexual abuse of women in the workplace.

Fearless Girl is a 4-foot high bronze statue of a young girl with her hands defiantly on her hips, promoting female empowerment. In 2017, a day before International Women's Day it was placed in front of the Bull of Wall Street sculpture, staring it down. That image went super viral around the world, and everybody was taking a photo of or selfie with the Fearless Girl.

State Street had commissioned the artwork to promote their index fund comprising 'gender-diverse companies that have a relatively high percentage of women among their senior leadership.'

Subsequently, State Street wanted to tour it around the world because the bank wants to show they're serious about gender equality in the workplace and they're serious about supporting women. Or something.

Unfortunately for them some security company in Sydney that nobody in America had heard of had already trademarked the word. Like a 4 foot girl standing in front of a charging bull, Calamity was standing in the way of one of the world's largest banks and they were having none of it.

Of course State Street's representatives could have picked up the phone to me and asked 'Could we could we borrow it or could we pay you some money?' It was after all a good cause and these types of trademark agreements are quite common between companies not in competition. A winemaker once wanted to produce a wine named 'Calamity' (our other trademark) and an agreement between our firms was hastily reached involving a handshake and a few bottles. Cheap.

However State Street didn't do that. Why would they bother when they've got lawyers on retainer? Instead they lodged a removal application with IP Australia (which I suspect they hoped we wouldn't notice meaning the trademark we'd used for 10 years would simply disappear).

Unfortunately for them, we did spot it and they learned what 'Fearless' actually means when we took them to court. More specifically, we had no choice but to do so in order to defend our trademark against a bank that wanted to engage in some corporate virtue signalling.

And ultimately we prevailed however it cost us a small fortune as cost orders are rare in these matters. As the plucky David to a corporate Goliath we spent this fortune trying to prevent a bank taking away something of ours that we had owned for over a decade.

At the time, nearly 45 percent of my company's workforce was female. Which is exceptionally high in the security industry, which is traditionally very blokey.

As well as disproportionately hiring women, my company helps women. We provide a number of services to female victims of domestic violence, including pro bono assistance to women's shelters and a variety of support tools to women at-risk. We have literally saved women's lives on multiple occasions.

My company, which was quite literally employing women at a rate far above industry norms and helps women at-risk daily was being hurt by a bank trying to promote corporate feminism and the hiring of women.

At the end of the day – this was hypocritical at best and antithetical at its worst.

It has often been my experience to date that the corporations that virtue signal the loudest in public are behaving the worst when they believe nobody is looking.

Vogue Magazine, who know a thing or two about women, wrote about State Street in October 2017[56]:

> *'In a depressing new show of faux feminism, State Street Corporation, the Boston-based bank that funded Wall Street's much-loved Fearless Girl statue, has been accused of paying its female and black employees less than their white male counterparts.. The multi-trillion-dollar asset management giant has paid a $5 million settlement to employees after a U.S. Department of Labour audit alleged that women in senior leadership positions at the company 'received lower base salaries, bonus pay, and total compensation since at least December 2010.'*

It gets better.

Michelle Ruiz wrote:

> *'In a potentially very hypocritical twist, State Street Corporation was reportedly notified of the audit's findings on March 31—*

56   Michelle Ruiz, Vogue Magazine 6 Oct 2017, 'State Street Corporation, the Financial Services Firm That Funded Wall Street's Fearless Girl Statue, Allegedly Paid Women and Black Employees Less.'

93

the same month it helped unveil the bronze Fearless Girl opposite Wall Street's famed Charging Bull, touting 'women in leadership, and the potential of the next generation of women leaders.' The installation—which has become a required stop for tourists, and women and girls in particular—was also part of State Street Corporation's support of the SHE Fund, a fund that invests only in companies with a declared commitment to gender diversity. All of this splashy, performative feminism, while the company allegedly was discriminating against the women and racial minorities in its own ranks.'

BLACK CLADDING AND TALKING THE TALK

The security industry provides a particularly helpful example of this double standard. If you visit the website of any large security manpower company they will talk all about their Indigenous Reconciliation Action Plan. They will have prominent acknowledgements of country on their website. They will talk about all about gender equity as well. Yet if you visit the sites to which they supply guards, you will seldom if ever see any Indigenous staff or females. What you will see are new arrivals from the Middle East, Africa and the subcontinent, nearly always male.

This was on-show during the disastrous Victorian Hotel Quarantine scheme - a failure which directly contributed to the deaths of over 800 people. Companies who specifically touted their Indigenous ownership or commitment to Indigenous matters, which would have been music to the Victorian Government's ears, were gifted the large contracts at a time most security companies were going to the wall. These large companies then subcontracted the work to smaller companies who subcontracted it again, to a level which at its bottom could be correctly characterised as modern slavery.

Sure, 800 people died but what price can you put on Diversity, Equity and Inclusion?

'Talking the talk' on their websites and in tender documents allows companies to pitch their DEI policies when bidding for lucrative government contracts worth billions, where walking the walk is apparently not considered important. In some cases, companies even erect an elaborate ownership structure so they can overnight purport to be 'Indigenous owned'. A similar concept known as 'black cladding' is where non-Indigenous businesses take unfair advantage of Indigenous businesses or individuals simply for the purpose of accessing otherwise inaccessible Indigenous procurement.

The Government of the day encourages this practice by throwing millions at such contracts in order to claim they're helping. This is despite doing virtually nothing tangible to close the gap within Indigenous communities, the way actually employing Blackfellas might.

'We pay our respect to hypocritical companies and to virtue signallers, past, present and emerging...'

Some companies will even 'say the quiet part out loud'. A recent marketing email I received was promoting personal protective equipment (PPE) for construction, such as reflective shirts and hard hats specifically with Indigenous artwork on it. The email gave the game away stating that wearing the artwork:

'will help to meet your APC (Aboriginal Participation in Contracts) spend and your DE&I initiatives'.

The clients who they list on their website include major state infrastructure projects and it's reasonable to guess why they're buying the product. If you guessed 'To help Indigenous Australians' you're naïve.

The clothing itself was manufactured in Bangladesh. A country not so much known for its Aboriginal population or its commitment to diversity – just ask the Rohingya refugees inside the world's largest refugee camp. Consider also the irony of producing work health and safety clothing for Australian workers, in a country where local workers routinely burn to death in fires at factories and depots.

Government agencies mandate a level of Aboriginal participation in contracts and buying shirts that were made in Bangladesh may help someone tick a box, meet a quota and passes for helping Indigenous Australians.

During the 2023 referendum campaign for The Voice, the *Yes* camp were selling t-shirts sporting official logos proudly stating they were 'printed in Naarm' (AKA Melbourne).

However the $40 T-shirts and $75 hoodies were also sourced from China and Bangladesh. Even the Yes Campaign wouldn't help local Indigenous trade.

No vote campaigner Warren Mundine suggested the true origin of the *Yes* merchandise was an example of the *Yes* campaign's elitism 'living off people's misery'. In an interview with the Daily Mail[57], Mundine said:

> *'These group of people are very elitist, very wealthy and all these corporations are used to having child labour in Bangladesh and all these other places. I am not surprised they are resourcing their stuff from some of the poorest countries in the world'*

---

57   David Southwell, Daily Mail, 17 August 2023, 'Voice to Parliament Yes campaign's merch is made in China and Bangladesh - despite saying it's printed in Australia on Naarm land"

THE LUKEWARM LINKEDIN EFFECT

When Covid was shutting down the world there was a handful of rare examples of racism towards Asian Americans. These arose from (reasonable) accusations that China had been responsible for Covid but sadly meant that someone who owned a Chinese restaurant in Manhattan risked getting abused by an idiot.

What happened was undoubtedly wrong. However while some tried to present these as proof of widespread American racism, these were statistically insignificant, highly isolated examples, akin to a few Sikh cabbies getting abused after 9/11. Despite which, on the tail of the now waning Black Lives Matter movement, woke virtue signalling corporations took this as an opportunity to move on to the next thing.

And on behalf of American Express, its CEO posted to LinkedIn. He sombrely said that he 'stands with all Asians!' He 'abhors racism against Asians and everybody should stand against racism towards Asians!'

And just like that, every high-net-worth Platinum Amex cardmember who was just about to duck down to the local Chinatown to punch a shopkeeper got the message.

Talk about a comment that didn't need to be made. I don't think there was a single sensible person who supports racism against Asians (or anyone else). Sure they might be out there, but I can't imagine they're very prolific on LinkedIn. Yet everybody dutifully cheered, clicking 'Like' on the CEO's post pushing it to the top of everybody else's LinkedIn feed.

I posted the following reply in the comments section:

'I agree with you that companies should absolutely fight racism against Asians. On that basis will American Express decline

to do business with companies that use Uighur slave labour (including violence against Asians) in Xinjiang Province in China?'

Unsurprisingly, my reply did not get many 'likes'. LinkedIn generally sees people avoid 'controversial' subjects they feel might impact their career. So posts like the CEO's entirely safe, inoffensive (and entirely redundant) example will get likes, but comments stating the obvious, like mine, will receive awkward silence.

However my private inbox suddenly filled with messages, including from a number of people who work inside American Express, some Asian. Each saying thank you. Comments included 'thank you for saying what so many of us feel' and 'Thank you for giving us a voice'.

I couldn't believe it. I had merely posted a smartarse reply to a virtue signalling CEO on LinkedIn and suddenly people felt I was giving them a voice.

I replied gratefully and asked each why they wrote to me in private, suggesting they say something in public where others could benefit from our dialogue. They each said the same thing. They believed agreeing (which they did) in public or even clicking 'like' could be a career limiting move.

I cannot say whether or not they would be punished for such views. I suspect their fears might be overstated (yet raises the question why they feel this way). However there is a technology driven fully-automated cancel culture which limits such common sense being more common. Especially where a lack of anonymity means to say certain things requires putting one's head above the parapet.

Every social media platform attempts to keep its users 'engaged' (read: Addicted) to keep consumers coming back over and over again for as long a period each time as possible.

Part of how they achieve this seems innocent enough. Giving users what it believes they might want.

If a person posts something and a lot of people click 'like' on that post, platforms like LinkedIn automatically think 'this is interesting. We should show this to more people'. Then those people click 'like', more people see and it spreads, sometimes virally. Conversely, if you only get a few likes, or none at all the platform assumes total disinterest and your post will be buried. This seems like a good idea but do you see the problem?

Post something saying 'We hate racism' and thousands of people will dutifully click 'like' and move on, the very same way they might on a photo of a friend's ugly baby. Whereas if you post something to that person saying 'You are also guilty of racism' that comment will attract silence and eventually die on the vine.

This has meant that banal virtue signalling rises to the top of the public discourse, if not the zeitgeist. Yet legitimate criticism gets hidden away. It is like a debating tournament held in a stadium where only one side has a microphone.

The content of posts by business leaders on LinkedIn is markedly different from what so many would say in private. In public they will play it safe and post harmless motherhood statements about social issues (which often have little to do with their business). Yet they will never, ever criticise the government of the day even when tax policies, industrial relations and economic management – things which absolutely impact business – are killing them. All things they'll happily talk about for hours over a drink in private.

ESG has also accelerated an environment where CEOs are encouraged, if not forced to act against their beliefs. This has created a perverse incentive at the corporate level. Once upon a time a Chief Executive's pay might be linked directly to share returns. Now as it is often linked to ESG metrics, there is a commercial incentive for them to take shortcuts in achieving these. For example offshoring labouring and environmentally destructive projects to countries where ESG rules simply don't apply, or where locals will simply look the other way.

Slave capital over there no longer matters because the ESG capital over here was worth far more.

CEOs will also blindly follow the crowd because that is how to score their next CEO job and keep being invited to cocktail parties. Like celebrities flown on a private jet to an island to discuss climate change. Nasty ideas like 'profit' are not discussed in polite company in a world of ESG.

While it's not a new problem to see Marxist ideology being taught to naïve undergraduate university students, that same ideology is now infecting MBA courses. Students, who will inevitably become senior executives and board members of large corporates, are not taught about how to shape a business but how business should shape everything else. Ideologies with their roots in Marxism have been rebranded for a cohort of aspiring MBA grand investment bankers with innocuous names such as 'Stakeholder Capitalism' or 'New Capitalism'. This is dutifully regurgitated by people who may have shied away from socialism on campus but have become Useful Idiots who will go and work in investment banks.

Remember however, none of these 'leaders', whose actions can greatly impact everybody's life, were elected.

ESG scores are not only allocated to large businesses they are increasingly being applied to small businesses whether they like it or not. And in order for the small business to receive work from a larger business it's no longer enough to be good and/or cheap. Now you have to use your ESG credentials to improve theirs. This will reach its absurd conclusion when a home-business achieving a high enough turnover will need to report on and consider its gender hiring policies. Even when it's a family business that had precisely zero say in how many boys and girls mum and dad had.

Small businesses have not yet realised what's heading down the pipeline but in due course with a push from the unelected 'leaders' at the World Economic Forum in Davos, ESG metrics will impact their every operation thousands of kilometres away. There are already start-up companies automatically assigning an ESG score, like a credit score to companies that never asked to be rated in this way, based on publicly available data.

US Presidential candidate Vivek Ramaswamy argued, in a post on X:

> '*BlackRock, State Street, and Vanguard represent arguably the most powerful cartel in human history: they're the largest shareholders of nearly every major public company (even of each other) & they use your own money to foist ESG agendas onto corporate boards – voting for 'racial equity audits' & 'Scope 3 emissions caps' that don't advance your best financial interests. This raises serious fiduciary, antitrust, and conflict-of-interest concerns.*'

One of those companies named certainly didn't advance my company's best financial interests!

Yet companies will continue to play along with this rather than say 'Enough'. Conrad Black, a regular attendee at Davos for years criticised the:

> '*...venality, cowardice and invertebrate tactical stupidity of much of the corporate world' which was neatly demonstrated by 'oil*

companies putting up slick television praising and purporting to
be part of the heroic march to a fossil-free world'.

This was a gleeful march toward corporate suicide
demonstrating a level of cognitive dissonance perhaps only
better exemplified by the so-called Queers for Palestine
marching in support of a culture that would murder them
given half a chance.

SO WHAT CAN BE DONE?

Currently, it tends to be billionaire business leaders who feel
safe to speak out in cancel culture. JK Rowling, the world's
most profitable author, will speak out about things. Elon
Musk will speak out about things. If they were cancelled,
they'd be crying all the way to the bank and wiping their eyes
with hundred-dollar notes.

I believe that the time has come where the quiet voices,
what used to be called the silent majority need to stop being
silent. But they need to be clever about it. It is fair to say that
some 'anti-woke' activists have become as loud, obnoxious,
and tedious as the woke-campaigners they oppose.

Somewhere in the middle, you've got a whole lot of
generally disinterested people. They are struggling to put
food on the table. They're struggling to pay their power bills.
The rights and wrongs of 'Drag Queen Story Time' at the
local council library probably is not the most important thing
on their mind.

In Australia, with its inherently undemocratic rule of
forcing everyone to vote, every few years they turn up
dutifully at the ballot. They simply haven't been represented
or engaged. And I feel business, with its loud voice has a

huge role to play here. The far Left's long march through the education system is now playing out in the boardroom.

What we all seem to be underestimating currently however is the critical mass which many of us have, if only we were to put our money where our mouths are.

If enough business leaders say 'enough is enough' to these absurd marketing fads and social engineering imposed by entirely unelected elites, they can put a stop to having every cause shoved down their throat - except the ones that will help their business survive.

Right now small businesses feel they can't say anything. However they're out there and there is a way you can spot them.

It's very easy to spot the virtue signalling companies. They put different flags in their foyer each month. Their email signatures which used to contain simply an email address, a phone number, and a logo are now 16 paragraphs long and contain gender pronouns applied by a corporate mail server whether the sender likes it or not.

If you want to identify a business who doesn't buy into the cult-like virtue signalling you can find them precisely because they're not saying anything. Their silence is instructive. They don't throw around words like 'authentic'. They just want to operate an authentically decent business. They deserve support. They deserve platforming, and they deserve to know that it's okay to just run a business. And to just do the right thing. And you don't need to get up and say things that simply do not need to be said, even though everybody else is doing it.

It's said 'An empty vessel makes the loudest sound, so they that have the least wit are the greatest babblers'. The babble online is deafening and we are worse off for it. Businesses are often on the receiving end of such online outrage. Many have never dealt with it and in their haste to avoid the mob, they take pre-emptive steps which are unwittingly playing right into the hands of people who would just as happily see their business fail. There's a reason not many businesses sponsor the annual Marxism Festival at Sydney University.

Businesses will increasingly require strength as the perpetually enraged voices often seem louder than they actually are. Companies will need to learn to tell the difference between genuine complaints from pissed off customers versus hundreds of emails magically generated by a single person who's never had a real job, sitting at their keyboard using AI software.

I loathe boycotts but instead propose a *buy-cott* of businesses quietly doing the right thing by their staff, shareholders and community, the way businesses used to, ahead of companies loudly proclaiming to do so.

All too often they're simply pretending.

THE WAY OF BEAUTY

Julian Porteous

ABSTRACT

*In the history of humanity, cultures and the moral structures that
underpin them have found their stability in a reference point beyond
themselves. They have some form of transcendental foundation. The
moral structures have, in their turn, defined the cultures and have been
a point of social cohesion. However, Western societies, whose foundation
has been based in Christianity, have now entered a stage of abandoning
such a reference point. Replacing the Christian worldview there is now
an emphasis on individual moral perceptions alone. This paper will
explore the cultural shift away from the transcendent. It will consider the
rise of the self as the moral point of reference.*

*It will then propose a path by which people may find a way back to
recognising the need for a transcendental point of reference. This is the
way of Beauty. The paper will consider the thought of Gerard Manly
Hopkins, Hans Urs von Balthasar and Joseph Ratzinger and their
understanding of the importance of Beauty as the Transcendental that
can lead to a discovery of Truth and Goodness, and ultimately of their
source in God.*

In the history of humanity cultures, and the moral
structures that underpin them, have found their stability
in a reference point beyond themselves. They have some
form of transcendent foundation. Whether it be the pagan
gods of Greece or Rome, or the 'noble truths' proposed by
Buddhism, or the articulation of Christian virtue inspired by

Sacred Scripture, societies have fashioned moral imperatives based in some form of transcendent order. The moral structures have, in their turn, defined the cultures and have been a point of social cohesion.

However, Western societies whose foundation has been based in Christianity, have now entered a stage of abandoning such a reference point. Replacing the Christian worldview there is now an emphasis on individual moral perceptions alone. Having largely abandoned the Christian vision of human life, society now tends to be directed by popular social movements, which are based more in emotion than reason and evidence. Such movements include, most notably extreme climate activism, the LGBTQI movement and its related 'diversity and inclusivity' activism particularly in the corporate and sporting area, and so on. Such causes have become of paramount importance in our society and are so compelling to the social elites that they are forcibly imposed. They tend to shift and change as society becomes caught up with new issues.

The LGBTQI movement has been very effective in using what at first glance appear as the innocuous concepts of 'diversity and inclusivity' to push its radical sexual and gender ideology across society. They have been able to push the culture from toleration of aberrant sexual and gender behaviour to affirmation. Not only does the media largely advocate the LGBTQI radical agenda, but we now see corporations and sporting bodies also pushing these agendas wanting to publicly prove themselves as 'in touch' and 'with it'. Thus, they have diversity and inclusivity policies and mandate training, the sporting associations have 'Pride Rounds'.

Moral thinking has been turned inward. It has not only become untethered from an orientation towards the transcendent, but has also discarded the need for a sound rational base. It is now grounded in the personal feelings an individual has about ethical issues. The moral order has become highly subjectivised.

In times past ethical codes were based in an order defined by the existence of a divine or transcendent reality. We acknowledged the existence of a higher objective or transcendent moral law which provided guidance as to how we should act in order to flourish or fulfil our nature. Our ethical beliefs were in this way teleology, they aimed at an end which was human flourishing. This approach understood that there was a greater purpose to human life than the mere satisfaction of desire and proposed the pursuit of virtue as a central moral ideal. It is through the development of the virtues that we are more easily able to do the right and good thing, through which in turn we flourish as human beings, and achieve our 'telos' or end. This was at the heart of Aristotelian ethics.

Christian moral teaching has its source in divine revelation expressed in the Sacred Scriptures. It draws, in particular, on the Ten Commandments and the moral teachings of Jesus. However, the Catholic Church teaches that we can come to understand the Divine moral law not just through divine revelation but also through what is called the natural law, which involves the use of human reason. Essentially the Natural Law is the participation in the Divine law through our use of reason. Through the natural law we can discern the primary moral precept that good is to be done and evil avoided, reflecting on human inclination we can then identify secondary precepts, which involve goods such as 'life', 'human reproduction', 'education' etc, and the promotion and protection of these goods. These moral precepts of the natural law are not limited by culture or custom. They belonged to all of humanity because all people were created by a wise and provident Creator.

Our society now has large numbers of people who do not believe in the existence of God or any transcendent reality and so we are moving from a transcendent frame of reference to an immanent frame of reference. Once the society no longer acknowledges the transcendent order as providing an objective basis for morality, anything becomes, in principle, morally acceptable and a properly ordered civilised society is no longer possible. Once a society no longer recognises and respects the existence of the objective moral law, there is only the law of the mob or the strongest and most powerful, and we can only move along the path towards societal collapse.

A number of social commentators have described this process. They have described it in various ways. They speak of the emergence of the 'imperial self', or the 'expressive self'.

One such commentator is Carl Truman who, in his book, *Rise and Triumph of the Modern Self,* speaks of Mimesis and Poiesis saying,

> *Put simply, these terms refer to two different ways of thinking about the world. A mimetic view regards the world as having a given order and meaning and thus sees human beings as required to discover that meaning and conform themselves to it. Poiesis, by way of contrast, sees the world as so much raw material out of which meaning and purpose can be created by the individual.[58]*

Drawing on the thought of Phillip Rieff he describes three types of worlds. The first was the pagan world with moral codes based on myths. The second world is where

---

58   Carl Truman, *Rise and Triumph of the Modern Self,* Crossway, Illinois, 2020, p.39

moral outlook is based on belief in a transcendent god. The third world has a moral outlook which is devoid of a transcendent element and so is based on nothing beyond the individual human person. Rieff further comments that this third worldview becomes an 'anti-culture' as it sees moral frameworks as oppressive and restrictive of human freedom. It readily dismisses the old moral values as impotent and not a little ridiculous.[59]

Truman maps out a path that humanity has taken as it has distanced itself from the Christian vision of life. He describes the emergence of the 'psychological self' which he traces back to the Enlightenment of the 18th century, citing among others, Jean-Jacques Rousseau (1712-1778) who said, 'all I need to do ... is to look inside myself'.

This is further advanced by the Romantic poets like Wordsworth, Blake and Shelley. Truman identifies an ethics based in aesthetics. It is what feels right that is right. Here Truman sees the seeds of the therapeutic culture where one's desires are paramount.

Truman describes the 'plastic self' where a person considers that they can make and re-make themselves as they wish.

With these changes in self-understanding so the way of moral thinking has changed. Ethics is now a function of feeling, devoid of rational thought. Such thinking is based in personal preference alone. Alasdair MacIntyre, in *After Virtue*, describes such an approach to ethics as *emotivism*.[60] What is viewed as morally good is simply what I feel is good. The goal of moral choice is seen as self-actualisation or self-

59   See Phillip Rieff, *Triumph of the Therapeutic: Uses of faith after Freud*, ISI Books, 2007.
60   See Alasdair MacIntyre, *After Virtue (3rd Edition)*, University of Notre Dame Press, 2007.

expression. Such patterns of thinking can become so self-preoccupied that it comfortably denies evident biological reality, as we see in the transgender movement.

When moral thinking becomes subjective an immediate effect is that moral living no longer has a communitarian dimension. Society is fractured into individual preferences. The notion of the common good evaporates. When this occurs we are in fact entering into an era of anti-culture. Moral debate in contemporary society is difficult because people have positions which are either transcendent or immanentist and there is no common ground upon which debate can be pursued. There is no longer a consensus on what constitutes the proper basis for morality.

In philosophical thought traced back to Plato and taken up in the Catholic intellectual tradition is the notion of three particular Transcendentals: Truth, Goodness and Beauty. They are called such because they are basic attributes of being, all things have these properties. Properly understood they exist perfectly in God. They are properties of the nature of God. So, God is Truth, God is Goodness, God is Beauty. They are attributes that all beings have to some extent, but exist perfectly in God. The Transcendentals give us glimpses into what is metaphysical or spiritual. They direct us towards something which is much more and beyond ourselves, perfection of being. Ultimately, they direct us towards God.

When we reflect on the mind of our contemporaries we note that the notion of objective truth and goodness is no longer affirmed and, as a result, no longer pursued. What about Beauty? While we can see that the ideal of beauty has been under attack in our society (we can think of *Dark Mofo* here in Hobart), there is perhaps some more basic inclination to beauty in the human person that has been harder to supress. It is evident to all that beauty exists as a quality that attracts. We cannot but be moved by the experience of beauty. I would propose that beauty is truly the radiation of God.

Let us pose the question, though, what makes something beautiful? How can we define beauty? This has intrigued both philosophers and artists alike. Edmund Burke attempted to grasp the nature of beauty by considering the question of proportion. In *A Philosophical Enquiry into the Origin of our Ideas of the Beautiful and the Sublime* he wrote:

Turning our eyes to the vegetable kingdom, we find nothing there so beautiful as flowers; but flowers are of every sort of shape, and every sort of disposition; they are turned and fashioned into an infinite variety of forms. ... The rose is a large flower, yet it grows upon a small shrub; the flower of the apple is very small, and it grows upon a large tree; yet the rose and the apple blossom are both beautiful. ... The swan, confessedly a beautiful bird, has a neck longer than the rest of its body, and but a very short tail; is this a beautiful proportion? we must allow that it is.[61]

The eighteenth-century philosopher, David Hume, took the view that beauty was rather in the mind of the beholder.

Beauty is no quality in things themselves: It exists merely in the mind which contemplates them; and each mind perceives a different beauty. One person may even perceive deformity, where another is sensible of beauty; and every individual ought to acquiesce in his own sentiment, without pretending to regulate those of others.[62]

61   Edmund Burke, *A Philosophical Enquiry into the Origin of our Ideas of the Beautiful and the Sublime, 1956,* https://www.gutenberg. org/files/15043/15043-h/15043-h.htm#A_PHILOSOPHICAL_ INQUIRY

62   David Hume, *Of the Standard of Taste,* 1757, https://home. csulb.edu/~jvancamp/361r15.html

This is the insight of philosophers who clearly struggled to define what makes something beautiful. What do poets think makes up the nature of the beautiful?

I would like to give some attention to the thought and writings of the Catholic poet, Gerard Many Hopkins. He was much engaged with the question of the nature of beauty. For him the source of beauty was God Himself. He writes in his poem, *God's Grandeur*, 'the world is charged with the grandeur of God'. He saw nature as replete with beauty and coined his own words to depict his understanding. He spoke of the way that the 'inscape' of a thing was 'instressed' upon the human faculties. For Hopkins there is a way of seeing nature that impresses its inner radiance on us. What is within nature will at times flame out, 'like shining from shook foil'. We all experience beauty. Even what may appear common has something wonderful to reveal to us, as Hopkins expresses it: 'There lives the dearest freshness deep down things'.

Hopkins is aware that the perception of beauty leads to a recognition of the Creator as its source. Let us allow his majestic movement of words and sounds in the poem *Pied Beauty* give us a moment to contemplate how the perception of beauty opens the soul to God:

> *Glory be to God for dappled things –*
> *For skies of couple-colour as a brinded cow;*
> *For rose-moles all in stipple upon trout that swim;*
> *Fresh-firecoal chestnut-falls; finches' wings;*
> *Landscape plotted and pieced – fold, fallow, and plough;*
> *And áll trádes, their gear and tackle and trim.*
>
> *All things counter, original, spare, strange;*
> *Whatever is fickle, freckled (who knows how?)*

With swift, slow; sweet, sour; adazzle, dim;
He fathers-forth whose beauty is past change:
Praise him.

Contemporary society needs a starting point to rebuild a consciousness of the transcendent and I would propose, along with Swiss theologian Hans urs von Balthasar and Joseph Ratzinger, Benedict XVI, that the appreciation of the beautiful is the place to begin.

Von Balthasar in his three-volume monumental work, *The Glory of the Lord*, begins with a theology focussed on the notion of beauty as a transcendental. He is convinced that we must start with beauty before treating of goodness and truth. He considers that the contemplation of beauty is to actually contemplate divine love. Beauty opens us to the glory of the Lord. When we encounter beauty we are drawn towards that which is beautiful but taken further towards the source of this beauty. We are taken beyond ourselves. This is what opens us up to the reality of the divine. Von Balthasar writes:

> *Beauty is the last thing which the thinking intellect dares to approach, since only it dances as an uncontained splendour around the double constellation of the true and the good and their inseparable relation to one another. Beauty is the disinterested one, without which the ancient world refused to understand itself, a word that both imperceptibly and yet unmistakably has bid farewell to our new world, a world of interests, leaving it to its own avarice and sadness.[63]*

The experience of beauty seizes the senses and causes a person to pause in wonder. Think of witnessing a glorious

63   Hans Urs von Balthasar, *Glory of the Lord: a theological aesthetics*, Vol 1, T & T Clark, Edinburgh, 1982, p 18.

sunset or a natural vista. When we see beauty, we are captivated and lifted beyond ourselves. The encounter with the beautiful can be like the wound of an arrow that strikes the heart and so opens our eyes to the deeper reality of things. Listening to a Bach Cantata, or gazing at an icon, or walking through a medieval cathedral, we are transported to another place. When we experience the great works of the Christian tradition that place is the place of faith. Somehow in this moment we are in touch with the divine.

There is, of course, a false beauty. Such 'beauty' may be dazzling or engaging but it does not take us out of ourselves, but rather locks us in within ourselves. It may stir up passions for power or pleasure. It is a deceptive beauty like the fruit that attracted Eve. It was 'delightful to the eyes', but was a temptation to turn from God.

Now let us turn our attention to the thought of Joseph Ratzinger. The notion of beauty long engaged his thinking. As Pope the theme was taken up in a number of his writings. For example, he said in 2002:

> *I have often affirmed my conviction that the true apology of Christian faith, the most convincing demonstration of its truth...are the saints and the beauty that the faith has generated.*[64]

Ratzinger is convinced that beauty will open people to discovering the faith. He comments in referring to young people who have become estranged from the faith, that 'a sacred image can express much more than what can be said

---

64   Joseph Ratzinger, *The Feeling of Things, the Contemplation of Beauty*, 2002, https://www.vatican.va/roman_curia/congregations/cfaith/documents/rc_con_cfaith_doc_20020824_ratzinger-cl-rimini_en.html

in words, and be an extremely effective and dynamic way of communicating the Gospel message.'[65]

Based on this conviction Ratzinger considered that beauty had a vital role in the celebration of the sacred liturgy. He is not proposing here a certain aestheticism, an elitist pursuit of perfection. Rather, he sees that beauty in the liturgy 'is not mere decoration, but rather an essential element of the liturgical action, since it is an attribute of God himself.' He encouraged priests to be more conscious of the *ars celebrandi*. *He is conscious that* the reverence of a priest, and the palpable piety with which he celebrates the Eucharist, can move the faithful to greater participation in the sacred mysteries.

In a homily at a Mass in St Patrick's Cathedral, New York, in 2008, Pope Benedict reflected on how the stained-glass windows in a great cathedral, which from the outside look plain and lifeless, yet when the light flows in from outside they are radiant in colour and beauty. He commented, 'It is only from the inside, from the experience of faith and ecclesial life, that we see the Church as she truly is: flooded with grace, resplendent in beauty, adorned by the manifold gifts of the Spirit.'

Pope Benedict XVI was convinced that it was beauty expressed in the liturgy that lifted the heart to worship of God. He commented, 'The beauty of the liturgy is part of this mystery; it is a sublime expression of God's glory and, in a certain sense, a glimpse of heaven on earth'.[66]

65   See Joseph Ratzinger, *Moto Proprio* of the Supreme Pontiff Beneidct XVI for the Approval and Publication of the *Compendium of the Catechism of the Catholic Church*, 2005. https://www.vatican.va/content/benedict-xvi/en/motu_proprio/documents/hf_ben-xvi_motu-proprio_20050628_compendio-catechismo.html

66   Pope Benedict XVI, *Sacramentum Caritatis*, no 35, 2007,   https://www.vatican.va/content/benedict-xvi/en/apost_

Pope Benedict saw the beauty captured in the authentic celebration of the liturgy as the 'radiation of God'. He expressed this in these words,

> *Like the rest of Christian Revelation, the liturgy is inherently linked to beauty: it is 'veritatis splendor.' The liturgy is a radiant expression of the paschal mystery, in which Christ draws us to himself and calls us to communion.*[67]

When beauty is in evidence in the celebration of the sacred liturgy, then it becomes the path to true worship of God. Beauty here is at the same time physical and spiritual, an intersection of the visible and the invisible. Modern society might have lost sight of a transcendent point of reference, but we cannot absolutely supress the human heart's desire for the divine and what is transcendent. The modern person struggles to find a way to the transcendent via the path of truth and even goodness. But there is hope and possibility in the way of beauty.

exhortations/documents/hf_ben-xvi_exh_20070222_sacramentum-caritatis.html

67   Ibid.

CREATING A CULTURE OF FREEDOM

John Roskam

It's a privilege to be speaking to you about 'Creating a Culture of Freedom'. The Christopher Dawson Centre for Cultural Studies led brilliantly by its director, Dr David Daintree has done a superb job at fulfilling its mission of promoting awareness of the Catholic intellectual tradition and securing the cultural patrimony of Western Civilisation.

I would like to do two things in my comments to you today. I will assess the condition of freedom in Australia today, and then I'll suggest how we might win back some of the freedoms we have lost in recent years. I will argue that we must begin that process by putting into practice the exhortation of Aleksandr Solzhenitsyn 'Live not by Lies'.

OUR LOST FREEDOMS

For too long Australians committed to freedom have consoled themselves believing that while the condition of freedom in this country is desperate, it's not yet serious.

As Christians lose their jobs, as Liberal and Labor governments embrace government censorship of our speech and opinions, and as the heritage that's created liberal democracy and the rule of law is obliterated, too many of us have shrugged our shoulders and uttered some variation of 'Oh well, it's always darkest before dawn,' or 'The tide will turn' or 'The pendulum will swing back.'

But a pendulum swung from one side to the other never returns to its original position.

We need to understand that in Australia, we're not losing our freedoms – we've already lost them. If you don't feel you're a free person, you're not. The institutions that once sustained our freedoms either no longer exist or are hostile to freedom.

More than three years of Covid is proof that the principles and practices of freedom are no defence against the government. Put simply, if the Australian public were ever to be given a choice between liberty and security, it is now clear which they would choose.

Remember, Daniel Andrews was decisively re-elected last year, and so was Mark McGowan in 2021.

Covid revealed Australians to be among the most obedient people in the world. If the arrest and handcuffing of a mother in her pyjamas in her living room in front of her screaming children for a social media post advertising a lawful protest don't arouse a population and its politicians, then probably nothing will. No matter what the circumstances, a free country is not one which doesn't allow its citizens to enter or exit.

One of the most perceptive historians of this country, John Hirst, wrote nearly twenty years ago about the myth we tell ourselves that we are easy-going, freedom-loving larrikins. 'The Australian people despise politicians, but the politicians can extract an amazing degree of obedience from the people, while the people themselves believe they are anti-authority.'

'Australians are suspicious of persons in authority, but towards impersonal authority they are very obedient.' Hirst argued government arrived here in 1788 fully formed, and whatever freedoms Australians once enjoyed were given to them, not won, and that because of our history, the state has been relatively benign. We, therefore, tend to assume the best, not the worst, of our rulers. The reality is that today in Australia, freedom is very much a niche interest. It goes without saying we're more free than, say, the residents of Hong Kong. Our elections are still free, and we can still choose who to vote for (even if our major parties are virtually indistinguishable from each other).

WINNING BACK OUR FREEDOMS

To say that 'freedom is lost' is not to suggest that freedom can't ever be regained. It can be, but it's much more difficult to win back something than to maintain a hold of it. If ever we are to win back our freedom, there are three things we must understand.

First, the way to freedom in Australia is not through politics. Andrew Breitbart was right. 'Politics is downstream from culture'. If we want to change our politics, we must first change our culture. The Liberal party is not a cultural institution; it has no interest in culture, and its influence on the country's culture in recent decades has been negligible. Unlike the ALP, which understands cultural power, the Liberals have done nothing to foster intellectual or policy support for either the party or its aims. When Liberal MPs claim their party should avoid the 'culture wars' it reveals just how far their party is removed from the battle for the Australian way of life. No Labor MP would ever say their party should only talk about economics. The Liberal party, just like any other civil institution, is a creature of a nation's culture. As Australia's culture has moved left, so have the Liberals. For nearly nine of the last ten years, the Liberals have been in power in Canberra, and freedom has retreated.

Bill Leak, Archbishop Julian Porteous, Israel Folau, Peter Ridd, Zoe Buhler, and Calum Thwaites are just some of the Australians either persecuted or prosecuted in recent years by either their employer or government authorities because of what they said or believed. Every episode occurred under a Liberal prime minister.

Unfortunately the Liberal Party is not the party of freedom. When the former prime minister Scott Morrison, as federal treasurer said in 2017 that freedom of speech 'doesn't create one job' he was simply saying publicly what many Liberal MPs believed privately. It's significant that after Morrison make his remarks, in the context of potential reforms to Section 18C of the Racial Discrimination Act there was no pushback from his colleagues. There was no groundswell of support for freedom of speech from Liberal MPs and against what Morrison said. In fact it was far easier to find examples of Liberal MPs arguing against changing Section 18C than to find MPs urging change. Too many Liberals seem to believe that 'culture wars' are a 'sideshow alley' as Peter van Onselen wrote in 2016. The left devotes as much effort to destroying our culture as it does to disparaging those who dare stand against what they are seeking to do. According to van Onselen 'activism on the left has increased in recent years, but the broader right shouldn't' take the bait', but what 'the right' should do he does not say. We are now starting to see the consequences of not fighting for our freedoms.

Last year I wrote about the experience of Andrew Thorburn, the former CEO of NAB who was forced to quite as the chief executive of the Essendon football club because of his religious beliefs. His is an important story because it reveals how it is becoming increasingly untenable for Christians to participate in public life in Australia and it also shows how the once 'safe space' of sport as a place where religious and political differences can be put aside has become a place of political contest.

If sport is life, then life in Australia is not in a good way.

The country and public life in the country has changed and has changed quickly. A decade of "diversity" and "tolerance" policies and slogans has made Australia less diverse and less tolerant. The country is close to becoming less recognisable by the day.

In the same week former NAB CEO Andrew Thorburn was forced to quit as the head of the Essendon football club in Melbourne because of his Christian beliefs, it was announced Haneen Zreika, a Muslim woman playing for Greater Western Sydney in the AFL, wouldn't participate in an upcoming game because she would have been required to wear a jumper representing a perspective conflicting with her religious beliefs.

Certainly there are nuances to both episodes. Some Australians will look around and see places where Christians can't work and Muslims can't play football. While it's true that both instances involve the AFL, what's happened is not very different to the discrimination meted out to people of faith by the NRL or Rugby Australia.

What the AFL once was has helped make it the most powerful cultural institution in the country. More powerful than political parties, big business, trade unions or any civic or service association – and definitely more powerful than organised religion. During Melbourne's COVID-19 lockdowns in 2020 when the Andrews government closed churches, mosques, synagogues, and temples, the MCG remained open for the AFL to continue to play its games and satisfy the requirements of its sponsors and broadcasters.

What's happened to Thorburn and Zreika reveals how public life in Australia is now hyper-politicised. The personal has truly become the political. Personal faith is no longer personal or private. What's expected of people like Thorburn and Zreika is a public profession of adherence to the prevailing cultural and political orthodoxy. Neutrality is not enough. In Thorburn's case not even his public support and championing of diversity initiatives when at NAB, irrespective of his personal beliefs, is enough for those who regard themselves as the arbiters of our cultural norms.

Thorburn is the volunteer chairman of City on a Hill, a network of Anglican churches. Its position on abortion and homosexuality sits firmly within the mainstream of orthodox Christianity – 'human life begins at conception, marriage is between a man and a woman and sex should be confined to marriage'.

According to the Essendon president, those positions are in direct contradiction to our values as a Club ... I also want to stress that this is not about vilifying anyone for their personal religious beliefs, but about a clear conflict of interest with an organisation whose views do not align at all with our values as a safe, inclusive, diverse and welcoming club'.

It's understandable a church would have a view on abortion. Why a football club should have one is less clear. The decline of religion hasn't meant moral viewpoints are enforced any less vigorously than they once were. On the contrary, morality is now enforced everywhere, all the time.

The precedent has been set. To be the chief executive of an AFL club requires successful candidates to hold and espouse a view (and the correct view) on abortion and marriage.

In exactly the same way these days the CEO of an Australian public company must have and affirm the correct view on matters such as climate change and an Indigenous voice to parliament. No doubt some people will welcome the developments in the AFL over the last few days as evidence of how diverse and tolerant Australia is becoming. Others will take a different view.

Next, we must appreciate that the institutions of education, the mainstream media, and civil society are all now unequivocally hostile to freedom. They cannot be renovated or 'recaptured'. The only alternative is to create new and alternative institutions. It's inconceivable, for example, that Australia's universities will tolerate, let alone embrace, genuine diversity of opinion – they are too far gone. There's no point attempting to 'reform' something irretrievably broken.

My colleague at the Institute of Public Affairs, Dr Bella d'Abrera has recently written of the National Curriculum,

What is currently being unleashed in classrooms across this country is about as far away from a traditional curriculum as you can possibly get. Rather, it is an anarcho-political manifesto which seeks to dismantle the entire edifice of the modern state of Australia by undermining its values and institutions.

The progressive educationalists are using their considerable institutional power to bring forth and legitimise radical ideas such as the notion that Australia is a fundamentally racist country, and that all of its institutions are smokescreens for racial domination. It introduces children to the fiction of 'systemic racism', as well as the racist concept of 'whiteness' being problematic.

For example the 'Sustainability Cross Curriculum' priority is doing significant damage to Australia's youth. It has become the gateway through which children are being introduced to concepts and ideologies that have nothing to do with looking after the environment in the true sense. They are schooled in environmental determinism, which is the concept that humans and their natural environment are interrelated, and that environmental factors such as climate change presuppose the success or failure of civilisations. The priority promotes the idea that a sustainable world cannot be achieved without a socially just world, and that the two are inextricably linked. Children are repeatedly asked to 'recognise that the interdependence of Earth's systems and values of diversity, equity and social justice are essential for achieving sustainability'.

Australia's universities are no longer places of debate and discussion (if they ever were). A survey commissioned by the Institute of Public Affairs in 2019 of 500 domestic Australian university students found 31 per cent had been made to feel uncomfortable by a university teacher for expressing their opinion, and 59 per cent believed they have been prevented from voicing their opinion because of the actions of others students.

Finally, we must think small and we must look to our own actions first. We are a dissident minority, and the forces arrayed against us are great. Justice, truth and human dignity might be on our side, but in practical terms, we're holding a butter knife while our opponents are in charge of an Abrams tank. Gramsci was right. It will be a long march back, and success will be measured in inches. Charles Handy put it this way – 'We cannot wait for great visions from great people, for they are in short supply. It is up to us to light our own small fires in the darkness.'

In a remarkable book first published in 1995, *Private Truths, Public Lies - The Social Consequences of Preference Falsification*, Timur Kuran explains how totalitarian regimes are sustained not only by terror and violence, but also a pervasive culture of mendacity. In Eastern Europe under communism, individuals routinely applauded speakers they disliked, joined organisations whose mission they opposed, ostracised dissidents they admired, and followed orders they considered nonsensical, unjust, or inhuman, among other manifestations of consent and accommodation.

'The lie,' wrote Alexander Solzhenitsyn in the early 1970s, 'has been incorporated into the state system as the vital link holding everything together, with billions of tiny fasteners, several dozen to each man.' He then asked rhetorically, 'What does it mean, not to lie?' It means 'not saying what you don't think, and that includes not whispering, not opening your mouth, not raising your hand, not casting your vote, not feigning a smile, not lending your presence, not standing up, and not cheering.'

In an essay entitled *The Power of the Powerless*, published clandestinely in 1979, Vaclav Havel speaks of a greengrocer who places in his window, among the onions and carrots, the slogan 'Workers of the World, Unite!' What, wonders Havel, is the greengrocer's motive? 'Is he genuinely enthusiastic about the idea of unity among the workers of the world? Is his enthusiasm so great that he feels an irrepressible impulse to acquaint the public with his ideas. Has he really given more than a moment's thought to how such a unification might occur and what it would mean?'

Our greengrocer displays the assigned slogan not to communicate a social ideal but to signal his preparedness to conform to the political status quo…

The brilliance of this parable lies in its insights into the pressures that kept individuals loyal to their inefficient, tyrannical regimes. Official repression met with the approval of ordinary citizens. Indeed, it was predicated on their complicity. By falsifying their preferences and helping to discipline dissenters, citizens jointly sustained a system that many found abominable. In Havel's own words, the crucial 'line of conflict' ran not through the Party and the people, but 'through each person,' for everyone was 'both a victim and a supporter of the system.'

Havel's observation found vivid expression in a banner hung, after the fall of the Berlin Wall, above the altar in an East German church: 'I am Cain and Abel.'

Solzhenitsyn is right - '[T]he simplest, most accessible key to our liberation [is] personal nonparticipation in lies! Even if all is covered by lies, even if all is under their rule, let us resist in the smallest way: Let their rule hold not through me!'

In *Nineteen Eighty-Four* Orwell makes a compelling statement about the power of the individual to hold true to themselves. For Big Brother, the 'heresy of heresies was common sense'. Winston asks himself, 'if both the past and the external world world exist only in the mind, and if the mind itself is controllable - what then?' But then he realises: they were wrong and he was right. The obvious, the silly and the true had got to be defended. Truisms are true, hold on that! the solid world exists, its laws do not change. Stones are hard, water is wet, objects unsupported fall towards the earth's centre. With the feeling that he was speaking to O'Brien, and also that he was setting forth an important axiom, he wrote:

Freedom is the freedom to say that two plus two make four. If that is granted, all else follows.

WOKISM RISKS A DESCENT OF WESTERN CIVILISATION INTO NIHILISM

Ramesh Thakur

ABSTRACT

Like the Overton Window of political possibilities, the 'opinion corridor' channels the range of acceptable speech. Step outside it and professional offence archaeologists will dedicate themselves full-time to investigation, mob denunciation and cancellation. This is where the power of the woke mob comes from. The pursuit of social justice animated by group rights and an expanding victimhood hierarchy and grievance industry has become a war on truth, science, facts, merit and achievement. The 'increasingly hegemonic set of ideologies' has infiltrated and captured the classroom, boardroom, public institutions and newsroom and morphed into cancel culture. It has been corrupted into a full-frontal assault on the values of empirical science, rationalism, and objective truth; and on the great social, cultural, literary and artistic progress made under the impact of the Enlightenment in exploring the full range of human emotions that originated in Europe. Criticism, ridicule, sarcasm, an alternative point of view to the orthodoxy – all these today can be interpreted by someone, somewhere, on some occasion, as microaggression, hate speech, making them feel unsafe, etc.

Yet, underlying prejudices, injustices, resentments and bigotry are not addressed by arresting and cancelling people, but by being confronted with evidence, data and logic. The Enlightenment taught us to reject inherited traits to assess people's worth, potential, dignity and value; to focus instead on their character, behaviour and accomplishments. Wokedom turns that on its head to insist that everything and everyone must be judged on their pigmentation and gender attributes, that every disadvantage of rank and income is the result of systemic privileges and discrimination. It is the degenerate prodigy of political correctness. Ideas that once seemed crazy but harmless, have captured culture- and economy-defining institutions. No one is responsible for what s/he himself did, but we are all responsible for what somebody else did decades and even centuries in the past.

This Manichean framing is erroneous and dangerous. We cannot have a society or constitute a community without a multitude of shared frames of reference and patterns of action. This is why the claim that subjective feeling and self-affirming identity must be given legal recognition and protection is an existential threat to society itself. And, because it is limited to Western societies, it is an existential threat to Western society. The control of language is crucial, with the wholesale banning of perfectly good words and their replacement with bizarre and ugly substitutes. The debate on language is not an argument about human rights, but over truth and science versus lies and dogma. The fightback must also begin with decolonising language from the Empire of the Woke.

I speak tonight as a proud Australian man of Indian heritage. I pay my respects to the Aboriginal communities that have lived here since Dreamtime; to the pioneers who established modern Australia as a stable and prosperous democracy; and to the visionary leaders who strove tirelessly to create a society that grants equal citizenship to everyone in a vibrant multicultural country. I seek no privilege not available to every Australian, but I claim every right available to any other Australian.

The pathology of wokism is illustrated only too well, if somewhat unfortunately but also ironically for the publicity it generated that led to an increased registration, that this annual colloquium was refused its traditional venue this year and had to be shifted to the Australian Italian Club of Hobart.

The solution to the problem comes from an example involving Oxford University. On 19 May, Pro-Vice Chancellor Martin Williams told students they must be prepared to 'encounter and confront difficult views, including ones they find unsettling, extreme or even offensive'.

In political science we talk about the Overton Window: the spectrum of political ideas the public can be persuaded to consider. Anything outside it is 'unsafe' for politicians to support, regardless of their individual preferences. This changes over time and ideas and policies once deemed beyond the pale enter the Overton Window and can be put on the agenda, like the 1967 referendum on ending White Australia policy.

The Swedes have an analogous concept of the Opinion Corridor. Step outside it in today's social media and digital age and dedicated offence archaeologists will refer your current and past transgressions for investigation to 'fact-checkers' (in reality, left-leaning arbiters of opinion and morals), swiftly followed by mob denunciation and cancellation. Their binary judgemental conclusions sit uneasily alongside the complexity and nuance of contested issues in the culture wars.

This is the power of the woke mob.

MEANING AND ORIGINS OF WOKE

Woke is defined thus by Merriam-Webster: 'aware of and actively attentive to important societal facts and issues (especially issues of racial and social justice)'.

The pursuit of social justice animated by group rights has become a war on truth, science, facts, merit and achievement.

The 'increasingly hegemonic set of ideologies' has captured the classroom, boardroom, newsroom, and public and professional institutions, and morphed into cancel culture. In a Kafkaesque self-parody, a study into the censorship of the transgender debate in British universities was itself censored by London's City University which confiscated the findings of Dr Laura Favaro and made her redundant after activists accused her of transphobia.

The focus on group-based equality of outcomes is fundamentally at odds with the reality of individuals' unequal abilities, work ethics, drives, ambitions, and accomplishments. Criticism, ridicule, sarcasm, an alternative point of view to the orthodoxy – all can be interpreted by someone, somewhere, on some occasion, as microaggression, hate speech, making them feel unsafe, etc. As Rowan Atkinson said, we live in 'a creeping culture of censoriousness' that, 'with a reasonable and well-intentioned ambition to contain obnoxious elements in our society, has created a society of an extraordinarily authoritarian and controlling nature'. Underlying prejudices, injustices, resentments, bigotry are not addressed by arresting and cancelling people, but by being confronted with evidence, data and logic.

The word 'woke' has roots in African-American sensibility, to denote a state of enlightenment on systemic privilege and oppression, and the power structures pervading every aspect of social, political and economic interactions. Lately it has been corrupted into a full-spectrum assault on the values of empirical science, rationalism, and objective truth; on the great social progress made under the impact of the Enlightenment that originated in Europe, and the accompanying efflorescence of literary and critical arts that explored the full range of human experience and emotions.

Martin Luther King's dream was that people would be judged not by the colour of their skin but by the content of their character. Wokedom turns that on its head. Everything and every person must be judged on pigmentation and gender attributes, every disadvantage of rank and income is the result of systemic privilege and discrimination, whether oppressor and victim are conscious of this or not. Hence the need for unconscious bias training, a very lucrative field if you can gate-crash it, where the merest hint of a dissenting question can be weaponised.

Wokeness is the degenerate prodigy of political correctness. It once seemed crazy but harmless, the product of shallow ideas, toddler tantrums and immature passion. Yet it's depressingly clear by now that those ideas have captured culture- and economy-defining institutions. Toby Young, founder of the Free Speech Union, holds 'the pink conquistadors' may not be in office but they are very much in power and populate most civic, political, corporate, media and sporting institutions in the professional-managerial ranks. While our societies are imploding in the obsession to become more diverse, China is quietly getting on with becoming more dominant.

In Victoria, the Liberal Party, comfortably ensconced on the opposition benches, expelled one of its own, Moira Deeming, because a woman MP must not engage in a robust defence of women's voice and rights. Queensland's Minister for Women (and Attorney-General) Shannon Fentiman insists: 'Anyone that (*sic*) identifies as a woman is a woman', demonstrating grammatical as well as biological illiteracy. Health Secretary Brendan Murphy holds the definition of a woman to be a contested space.

UK Labour leader Sir Keir Starmer has been on track in the opinion polls for a landslide win in the next general election in 2025. Sir Keir is, shall we say, gender recognition fluid, as shown in this selection of some of his statements over time:

- November 2020: 'Trans rights are human rights';
- June 2021: 'We're committed to updating the GRA [Gender Recognition Act] to introduce self-declaration for trans people';
- September 2021: it is wrong to say 'only women have a cervix';
- March 2022: Refused multiple times to answer the question if a woman can have a penis;
- December 2022: still committed to reform the GRA to permit self ID;
- March 2023: After the debacle of the Gender Recognition Bill in Scotland that precipitated Nicola Sturgeon's demise, Labour strategists warned the UK election will be lost 'on day one' if Starmer doesn't change is position on trans rights;
- 1 April 2023: '99.9 per cent of women haven't got a penis'.

The number of women in England is around 30mn. By Starmer's understanding, therefore, in England alone there are 30,000 women walking around with a penis dangling between their legs. And this is the man who would be PM of the UK.

Keir's vaccilation has spread to his ideological colleague PM Chris Hipkins of New Zealand. Broadcaster Sean Plunkett asked him at a press conference on 3 April, in light of the kerfuffle during Posie Parker's visit and Keir's comment that 1 in 1,000 women have penises, to define a woman. He replied: 'I wasn't expecting that question so it's not something I have formulated, pre-formulated an answer on'. JK Rowling tweeted: 'In the interests of balance, someone should now ask women how they define Chris Hipkins'.

On 28 March, the Strategic Advisory Group of Experts of the World Health Organisation (WHO) issued a revised roadmap for prioritising the use of Covid vaccines that refers to 'pregnant persons'. Why would we accept this organisation as an authority on medical science and take any of its medical advice seriously?

Sex-based differentiation is observable at every level of biological function. Each of the 30 trillion cells that make up the human body has a nucleus containing 23 paired chromosomes. Of these, 22 are the same for males and females and are called autosomes. The 23rd pair is the sex chromosomes. Females have two copies of the X chromosome (XX), and males have one X and one Y chromosome (XY).

- A man has a penis, testicles, chest, and ejaculates sperm.
- A woman has a vagina, ovaries, eggs, breasts, womb, menstruates during a substantial period of her life, and conceives, gives birth and breast-feeds.
- On average, men and women differ in height, weight, strength, speed, endurance, facial features, bodily hair...

THE VOICE

The Voice is part of the Woke agenda in the sense that to be a good Australian is to support the Voice. This confuses feeling good about one's own virtue with doing good for the Aborigines. The obverse of sacralisation of the Voice is to vilify opponents as wicked racists. In contrast to emotional manipulation of guilt for historical wrongs, the case for No is reasoned, evidence-based and principled in rejecting the re-racialisation of Australia's governance construct. It will codify the grievance of the present generation of activists and be weaponised by successor generations to pursue ever more radical agendas. Yet the disconnect with practical deliverables will ensure its failure to expiate white guilt.

I oppose the Voice without qualification and apology because I oppose racial discrimination in any form and against any and all groups. As well as viscerally offensive in principle, constitutionalising a race-based lobby group will be divisive in practice, injecting the poison of race-based preferences into the constitutional heart of Australia's body politic while empowering and enriching a small coterie of self-serving activists, grifters, and race-baiters. It will give rise to a rent-seeking class of activists, split Aboriginal communities just like it has already split their leaders and jurists, introduce further difficulties in the path of legislation and implementation of executive decisions, and open the door to judicial adventurism.

Furthermore, the Voice will create an expanding bureaucracy seeking ever rising budgets. For, the most powerful tool yet invented by mankind to make any social problem permanent, is to give it its own permanent bureaucracy. The Canberra-based new department supporting the Voice will depend for its continued existence on proving that the problem is not yet solved. Indeed, it will make every effort to grow its own size, budget, powers and influence in the total machinery of government by identifying fresh areas of concern that should be brought within its jurisdiction. This is nothing peculiar to Aboriginal people or affairs. That's how bureaucracies work. Just look at how the DIE (diversity, inclusiveness and equity) industry has entrenched itself in every institution in the public and educational sectors, businesses, media and even sporting codes.

Authoritarianism advances through a reliance on vilification-cum-intimidation and the compliance of a majority that shrinks in shame and cowers in fear. Wider currents across the Western world have seen whites accused of deep-seated, irredeemable and systemic racism, the beneficiaries and carriers of white supremacy; statues toppled; curricula decolonised (which in practice means the erasure of white history, success, identity and culture); and dissenters cancelled. The zeitgeist encourages the romanticisation of non-Western cultures and history and the demonisation of everything European. You can praise any culture in the world except Western but must blame only Western culture for all the world's ills. We are creating a society in which no one is responsible for what s/he himself did, but we are all responsible for what somebody else did decades and centuries in the past.

How many schoolchildren are being taught to be ashamed of Australia's British heritage for the alleged institutional racism, dispossession and oppression, even though guilt is not inheritable? Weaponising the therapy language of safe spaces seems to require turning non-Caucasian populations and whites into permanent victims and oppressors. It should be possible, surely, to recognise and celebrate the contributions of Aboriginal culture and legacy on their own terms, without denigrating those of Europeans.

In an important speech in Parliament in May, Peter Dutton spoke glowingly of 'a success story like ours, one of Indigenous heritage, of British inheritance and of migration and multicultural success – three threads woven together brilliantly and harmoniously'. Recall the brouhaha last November over an innocent question from Lady Susan Hussey based in curiosity about Ngozi Fulani whom she met at a reception hosted by Queen Camilla. Fulani, a British citizen with parents from the Caribbean, wore flamboyant African clothing, headgear and necklace, yet took performative offence at being asked where she was from. The horror!

On my return from Tokyo the same week as Dutton's speech, my driver in the private transport from Brisbane International to Ocean Shores had a Turkish name. He was of similar age. My question where he was from originally, led to a an extended and mutually rewarding conversation about our respective origins, the diasporic spread of our siblings and their children, the location and occupation of our own children, the number of grandchildren and our hopes for their future in this wonderful land of equal opportunity.

Contrast that with this story in *The Australian*, still in the same week, by Seja al Zaidi, a journalist in Sydney, about a British-Asian woman. She berated an immigrant taxi driver for asking where she was from, uploaded her interaction to TikTok thereby putting the poor man's livelihood at risk, and complained about feeling incredibly 'unsafe'. Attributing racist malice to a curiosity-based conversation starter is evidence of just how an offence-seeking attitude poisons the well of social harmony in a truly multi-ethnic country whose PM is a Hindu of Indian origin (and Scotland's First Minister is a Muslim of subcontinental descent).

'HER PENIS': WHOSOEVER CONTROLS THE LANGUAGE
CONTROLS THE NARRATIVE

What does 'indigenous' mean?
- First inhabitants?
- Anyone born here?
- What of a sixth generation South Australian of Irish descent? Is she indigenous Irish but not Australian?
- Conversely, does an Australian Aborigine, born in Ireland of ancestors who went there six generations ago, remain an indigenous Australian?

Whoever gets to be gatekeeper to this question gets to determine the allocation of power and resources dedicated to the Aboriginal communities. Actor Tasma Walton, for example, has done a DNA test which shows she has 93 per cent British ancestry and seven per cent 'unknown heritage'. She claims Aboriginal ancestry from her mother's side who, she believes, was taken from her Victorian clan and brought to Western Australia. On that basis, she is seeking to join others linked to the Frankton-based Bunurong Land Council over competing claims from the Boonwurrung Land and Sea Council over 13,000 sq/km of territory. The courts will decide which of the two is the rightful representative of the Boonwurrung people, whether a woman called Eliza Nowan was a member of this clan, and whether Walton is descended from Nowan.

The UK Ministry of Justice has decreed that convicted criminals must not be called 'convicts'. Instead, they are 'persons of lived experience'. Meanwhile paedophiles are 'minor-attracted persons'. God help us.

Another manifestations is censorship. The word 'censor' has itself been replaced by 'sensitivity reader' as failed writers re-write some of the most successful writers in history, from Enid Blyton and Roald Dahl to Agatha Christie and PG Wodehouse. In this Orwellian-*cum*-Alice in Wonderland world where words mean exactly what the High Priests of Woke say, 'exclusionary, intolerant of different views and full of hate' becomes 'inclusive, celebration of diversity and full of love'. What's more, if you disagree with me, you are my enemy and have no rights and therefore I have the right to expel you from polite society, take away your livelihood, cancel you and disappear you like they did in apartheid South Africa and totalitarian communist countries.

A lot of gender reassignment surgery is nothing less than surgical mutilation. Yet in our twisted world, 'gender affirming' sounds not just innocuous but actually positive, whereas 'female genital mutilation'? What exactly is the difference between the two? On second thoughts, strike that question – I don't really wish to know.

The US produces more wokery than can safely be consumed at home and exports its surplus to the UK and Australia. This is well exemplified in 'People of Colour'. It is racist, offensive and insulting, implying there's white folk, and also-rans.

It's also empirically wrong. We are not a monolithic cohort to be classified at the whim of the Caucasians who make up a small fraction of the world's population. I'm happy to be called any one of Australian, Indo-Australian, Australian of Indian origin, Indian, or Asian. We don't call Caucasians 'People of No Colour'. Besides, 'whites' are the real 'people of colour': pink when born, red when sunburnt, blue when cold, purple when bruised, grey when dead, and supposedly yellow with fear and green with envy.

BIOLOGICAL REALITY VS TRANS IDEOLOGY

Who among the icons of the movement's pioneers would have believed that in the 2020s feminists would be fighting over the right to call themselves women? The anti-scientific push has taken such a turn that those who insist biology trumps ideology get punished: speaking biological truth to gender power is hate speech. Pride is fascism with a rainbow flag.

The best riposte to such idiotic rubbish is: 'I too was a man trapped inside a woman's body. Then I was born'.

The perverse but predictable consequence is that the wilful suspension of biological reality with pretend facts is a threat to women. That is, *women's rights would not be under threat if transwomen were honestly described as biological males and correctly 'pronouned'.*

Transwomen do not have the right to colonise all women's sports and spaces. The war against women's identity, rights, privacy and dignity is lost once you accept the science fiction of addressing as 'she/her', a 6'3' bearded man with a functioning male organ which he will proudly display in a woman's spa, regardless of how embarrassed, offended and unsafe the girls and women in there might feel. As for relabelling 'vagina' as a 'bonus hole', as recommended recently by Jo's Cervical Cancer Trust (!) in the UK, this linguistic outrage is about as offensive, degrading, hateful and hurtful as you can get. Is the Trust staffed by giggling adolescents? When I first read of it I was confident this was misinformation but no, it was a serious proposal. Where is John McEnroe with his fiery 'You cannot be serious!' eruptions when we – or rather, all the women of the world – need him? Come back, all is forgiven.

Even when media reports are critical of such stories as convicted rapists being housed in female prison wards, they go along with the pretence that the culprit is a 'she'. Not to mention the brilliance of the circular logic that reports of a rape in a female hospital ward were false because no men were present in the ward – when CCTV footage showed a trans 'woman' was indeed present.

In 2016, Dana Rivers, a once-feted campaigner for *'trans rights'*, brutally murdered a middle-aged lesbian couple and their teenage son in Oakland, California. Last week, after years in custody and countless legal delays, Rivers (formerly known as David Chester Warfield) *was finally sentenced to life without parole*. And then came a particularly grim twist. This male killer of two women was sent to a *women-only prison* to live out his days. If anything captures the dangerous grip gender ideology now has over American public life it is surely this: a man who murdered a lesbian couple being sent to a women-only jail. And what makes it worse is that the Rivers trial has almost been completely ignored by the wider media, activists and politicians. (Jo Bartosch, Spiked, 25 June 2023).

NIHILISM

Nihilism is defined by the Cambridge Dictionary as: 'A belief that all political and religious organisations are bad, or a system of thought that says that there are no principles or beliefs that have any meaning or can be true'.

The root of the pronouns pathology is the terminological sleight of hand in legally reclassifying 'born male' as 'assigned male at birth'. For, the purpose of a birth certificate is to *record* the objective sex of the newborn baby, not to assign a subjective gender to the baby based on the parents' prejudices and mental health issues. This leads directly to the pathology of preferred pronouns into wich the masses have been conned by the insistence that it is but a small act of kindness that costs us nothing but may save vulnerable people from ideationing or committing suicide. Watch this editorial monologue from Megyn Kelly and circulate it widely. It's hard to imagine how it can be bettered. And all in under 18 minutes.

We cannot have a society or constitute a community without shared frames of reference and patterns of action. Pronouns are a social-linguistic device for objectively differentiating males from females, not a matter of subjective individual preference. The claim – that subjective feeling and self-affirming gender identity must be given legal recognition and protection – is an existential threat to society itself. Because it's limited to Western societies, it is an existential threat to Western society.

There is good reason to create women-only spaces in toilets, changerooms, refuges, crisis services, prisons and sports. Efforts to use the full force of the law to coerce and compel everyone to genuflect to biologically false facts is reminiscent of communist totalitarian systems where people must show obeisance to party diktats or risk the public humiliation of show trials, confession of errors and spells in re-education camps.

How many victims will it take before authorities move to protect women prisoners from manipulative and abusive male predators? How many children will be sacrificed on the altar of the ideology of gender altering surgery before the medical profession calls a halt?

After the chaotic scenes of violence in Auckland, Posie Parker cancelled the scheduled Wellington event and instead returned home, having feared for her life because the NZ police were conspicuous by their absence, not there to control the mob venting its fury at women who dare to have a voice. The 'nation that prides itself on having been the first to give women the vote is now rather more looking like the latest to give women the boot'.

That's not the *ugly* face of trans 'rights activists' – it's their true face. To fight for trans *feelings* is to actively jeopardise the hard-won *rights to a safe and dignified life* of women.

Posie Parker's demand can be summed up as: 'Let Women Speak'. The trans mob's reply is equally pithy: 'STFU'.

THE CULT OF VICTIMHOOD AND MARTYRDOM

The self-righteous, self-congratulatory, juvenile trans-idiot who doused Parker in tomato juice in Auckland, justified her actions thus: Parker 'is advocating for our genocide and I want her to be full of blood'. By promoting the cult of victimhood, martyrdom and vengeance, they are veering dangerously close to terrorist rhetoric and actions. It's a logical culmination of violence, hatred and threats directed at anyone who questions the radicalisation of the self-ID agenda, most prominently JK Rowling. She has had to face threats of rape and murder, threats for which no one has so far been charged.

In this transformation of perpetrators of violence into victims of oppression, the characterisation of critics as Nazi torturers and enablers is an *essential* tool of justifying the intolerance, hate and violence directed at them by the trans activists.

AN INFLEXION POINT IN THE CULTURE WAR AGAINST WESTERN CIVILISATION

We are at an inflexion point in the culture war against Western civilisation. The ultimate goal of the culture warriors is to change the face of society by replacing the concerns of the majority (family-centred prosperity, growth, opportunity, decent housing, kids' education, old age pension) with their newer priorities (race, gender, decolonisation).

These radical ideologies have lain dormant but are now metastasising dangerously fast. The intention is to make challenging their ideology functionally and then statutorily illegal (for example, by outlawing 'deadnaming'), barring opponents from participation in civil society and banishing them from the public square.

'Gender-neutral' language is neither neutral nor inclusive but anti-woman. It erases more than half of humanity as a distinct category and excludes their rights to safety, dignity and privacy. Preferred pronouns are the poster child for the woke movement that's seldom right but always certain. How can you possibly refuse someone you call 'she/her' the right to use a woman's toilet or changeroom and compete in a women's swimming competition?

Yet in the Alice in Wonderland world in which we have allowed ourselves to be trapped like frogs in water brought ever so gently to the boil, a UK teacher was sacked for 'misgendering' a pupil. Maths teacher Joshua Sutcliffe believes biological sex is immutable and refused to address a female pupil who identifies as male with her preferred pronouns and included her in saying 'Well done girls'. In May the Teaching Regulation Authority convicted him of refusing to treat the student with due 'dignity and respect'. Pause a moment to think about the enormity of this case: the state can compel you, on pain of being fired, to speak a biological lie.

Transgender athletes – biological males asserting they are women to compete against females – are cheats. Women's sport was not created as a separate category for males who cannot cut it in men's competition. Nor was it to affirm identity but to ensure fair competition and, increasingly, equal prize money. And if they stand on the medallists' podium, they are also thieves with no shame who have stolen the honour, recognition, prize money from the female competitors – and their dreams, hopes and ambitions.

It breaks my heart to see girls and women lose out on these opportunities. Does it break yours?

The debate on trans language is not an argument about human rights, but over truth and science versus lies and dogma in epistemology. In a matching vein, it is not about the hurt sensibilities of men in dresses pretending to be women, but about the control of women's bodies and safe spaces by men. The control of language is central to this effort. This is why I propose we turn DEI into DIE at every opportunity.

THE SECOND COMING OR THE FIN DE SIÈCLE
OF WESTERN CULTURE

Rarely can WB Yeats' warning in *The Second Coming* have been so apposite:

The blood-dimmed tide is loosed, and everywhere
The ceremony of innocence is drowned;
The best lack all conviction, while the worst
Are full of passionate intensity.

Too many have been cowed into silence and go along meekly with males sexually appropriating the vulnerability of women, *the better to exploit, exclude, and prey on women*. It speaks to the power of men to deny the essence of womanhood. None of this would be possible without first denying that sex is a biological fact that cannot be subsumed under gender as a social construct.

But is 'some revelation at hand'? In the US, outraged parents are wresting back control from ideological extremists who have captured school boards, even if, remarkably, the Biden administration threatens to send the FBI against these 'domestic terrorists'. In the UK, the trans self-ID issue brought down Nicola Sturgeon in Scotland, and outfits like Stonewall, Tavistock transgender clinic and trans charity Mermaids suffered major setbacks after coming under public scrutiny. PM Rishi Sunak has committed to inserting 'biological sex', as a protected category under the Equality Act, to make it easier to maintain women-only spaces and sports.

On 30 April, at a Starbucks outlet in the UK, a transwoman employee is seen in a 56-second video clip berating a middle aged female customer for being transphobic, refusing to serve her, instead ordering her to leave the store, and assaulting the person who was filming the encounter. Starbucks sacked the employee. The encounter is a teachable moment:

- The man was aggressive, violent and emotionally unstable;
- Regardless of how they 'self-identify', these males have not shed their physical aggression and are quick to use their advantages of height, size and strength to abuse and intimidate women;
- It's all and only about what they want, rarely about reciprocal consideration, courtesy and civility;
- The prompt sacking of the rude employee is a welcome rarity.

Are we in Australia prepared to fight back? Are *you* prepared to fight back?

CONTRIBUTORS

Kenneth Crowther is a PhD candidate in literary and cultural history at the University of Southern Queensland, examining the syncretic nexus of humoralism, demonology, and meteorology in the plays of William Shakespeare and John Webster. After teaching for thirteen years in the secondary and tertiary sectors, he is now an independent consultant working in classical education and operational strategy, with a current engagement to help set up St John Henry Newman College, an independent classical Catholic school proposed for Brisbane. He lives with his wife and four daughters near Toowoomba, Queensland.

Kevin Donnelly. Since first warning about the dangers of politically correct language control and group think in the mid-1990s Dr Kevin Donnelly has established himself, in the words of Sky News' Peta Credlin, as 'one of Australia's foremost cultural-left warriors'. Kevin is a vocal defender of Western civilisation and Judeo-Christianity against the destructive and nihilistic impact of neo-Marxist inspired woke ideology. He writes regularly for the print and digital media, including: The Australian, The Daily Telegraph, The Catholic Weekly, Quadrant, the Australian Spectator and the London based Conservative Woman.

Kevin also appears regularly on Sky News and books published include *The Dictionary Of Woke, Cancel Culture and the Left's Long March, Christianity Matters In These Troubled Times* and *How Political Correctness Is Destroying Australia.* Kevin is a senior fellow at the ACU's PM Glynn Institute and his website is kevindonnelly.com.au

Fiona Mueller's extensive teaching background in foreign languages, English and History includes roles in Anglican, Catholic and government schools in Australia, Europe and the United States. Her interest in policy led her to the NSW Board of Studies (now NESA), followed by doctoral research in single-sex education. With experience gained at two universities, she became Head of ANU College at the Australian National University, during which her leadership and research were recognised in her appointment as a Senior Fellow of the Higher Education Academy (now Advance Higher Education) based in York, UK. In 2016 she joined the Australian Curriculum, Assessment and Reporting Authority (ACARA) as Director of Curriculum, a national role requiring collaboration with education authorities across all sectors and participation in national and international projects. Fiona is now an Adjunct Fellow at the Centre for Independent Studies. In April 2022, she was appointed to a three-year term on the ACARA Board as the nominee of the Australian Government.

Deidre Clary is a former English teacher and deputy principal in Australian secondary schools. During the first of several lengthy sojourns in the United States, she completed a doctorate at the University of South Carolina, subsequently being appointed to teach English and literacy in the College of Education. Her more recent work with aspiring teachers included supervision of secondary English interns and teaching online in the Master of Education program at the University of South Carolina (ranked #10 in the

US). Additionally, Deidre conducted school accreditation for the South Carolina Independent Schools Association. Deidre spent several years as a lecturer and researcher at the University of New England (Australia) where she is an Adjunct Lecturer. She has developed a special interest in the English language requirements of other academic disciplines, critical literacy and new literacies. In 2016-2017, Deidre supported research and international curriculum comparison studies to inform the latest review of the Australian Curriculum. She is an occasional writer with the Centre for Independent Studies.

Mrs Karina Hepner has over 25 years' experience as an educator in Australia, Canada and France in the areas of English, History, French and teacher librarian. Her qualifications include a Bachelor of Education (secondary) and a Master of Arts (Literature). In her spare time, she is a novice calligrapher. Most significantly, she is a mother to two sons, now fine young men.

Daniel Lewkovitz is the CEO of leading Australian security business Calamity (http://www.calamity.com.au). A libertarian by nature he is one of a handful of business leaders who is outspoken in public and critical of government impingement on personal freedom and private business. He has attracted thousands of followers on LinkedIn who frequently message him in private to apologise that they can't publicly agree with him for professional reasons. Daniel stood in the last Federal election in the high profile, yet unwinnable seat of Wentworth with a specific goal of getting nuclear energy on the national agenda.

Sarah Flynn-O'Dea has Bachelor of Arts, Science, and Psychology honours as well as a Graduate Diploma in Secondary Education. She has spent many years in education as a secondary teacher and has observed the increasing tension and conflict in schools wrought by activist ideology and a fragmented post-modern anthropology. It is in this context that she promotes the tradition of Classical education as a potent alternative framework for mainstream education. Sarah founded *Logos Australis* in 2021 with a mission to promote Classical education in the Liberal Arts Tradition in Australia. She is a founding member of the Australian Classical Education Society and produces and distributes articles, content and curriculum to progress her mission. Sarah is a mother of 5 children and an avid gardener, reader, a traditional folk musician and nature lover.

Archbishop Julian Porteous was ordained a priest for the Archdiocese of Sydney in 1974. In 2002 he was appointed Rector of the Seminary of the Good Shepherd in Sydney. In 2003 he was named Auxiliary Bishop of Sydney by Pope St John Paul II and was ordained by Cardinal George Pell at St Mary's Cathedral, Sydney in September 2003. A decade later Archbishop Julian was installed as Archbishop of Hobart in September, 2013. He has always been actively involved in evangelisation, particularly among young people, and was instrumental in establishing the Pastoral Training School (now known as the Summer School of Evangelisation) which, since 1984, has formed thousands of young Catholics in their Catholic faith and in the pastoral skills necessary to contribute to the Church's evangelising ministry. He actively promotes the role and work of the new ecclesial movements as a grace given to the Church in our time to renew the Catholic faith and promote the evangelising mission of the

Church. He also established CRADIO, a digital radio service which promotes the New Evangelisation through the new media, now associated with Parousia Media.

John Roskam is a Senior Fellow at the Institute of Public Affairs, where he was Executive Director from 2005 to 2022. He is the co-author of 'Magna Carta - The Tax Revolt That Gave Us Liberty' and a contributor to numerous essay collections including 'Blaming Ourselves - September 11 and the Agony of the Left', 'Liberalism and the Australian Federation', and 'The Great Labor Schism - A Retrospective'. He has a fortnightly column in The Australian Financial Review and he writes weekly at 'One & Free' at Substack.

Ramesh Thakur is Emeritus Professor in the Crawford School of Public Policy, The Australian National University and a Brownstone Institute Senior Scholar. A former United Nations University Assistant Secretary-General and educated in India and Canada, he has held full-time academic appointments in Fiji, New Zealand, Canada, and Australia and been a consultant to the Australian, New Zealand and Norwegian governments on arms control, disarmament and international security issues. Ramesh was a Commissioner and one of the key authors of The Responsibility to Protect; Principal Writer of Secretary-General Kofi Annan's second reform report; and Foundation Director of the Balsillie School of International Affairs in Waterloo, Ontario. His books include Global Governance and the UN, The Group of Twenty (G20), The Oxford Handbook of Modern Diplomacy, The United Nations, Peace and Security, and The Nuclear Ban Treaty. He was Editor-in-Chief of Global Governance and is a founder of Australians for Science and Freedom.

www.ingramcontent.com/pod-product-compliance
Lightning Source LLC
Chambersburg PA
CBHW052012030426
42334CB00029BA/3186